The Hawai'iana Project

The Hawai'iana Project

Edited by Susan Kilbride

The Hawai'iana Project

The Hawai'ian feather helmet on the front cover is courtesy of the King Kamehameha Hotel in Kona, HI

Distributors and retailers can purchase this book directly from the publisher at:
www.createspace.com/info/createspacedirect

ISBN-13: 978-1483937564

ISBN-10: 1483937569

To the people of Hawai'i,

for all that you have given us.

Thank you

Acknowledgements

So many people have helped us with this project that I am afraid to list them all here in case I forget someone. My students and I have spent the last year going to every Hawai'ian festival that we could find, meeting with people on field trips, taking classes, and doing everything we could to learn more about the Hawai'ian culture. During that time, we have met and spoken with many wonderful people who were willing to share their expertise with us. Thank you all for your support and kindness.

And a special thanks to my students' parents. We couldn't have done it without you.

Note to the Reader

This book is written by the students in my homeschooling newspaper class. The assignment was to write three or more Hawai'ian cultural articles that had a "hands on" element in them. I wanted the students to not only practice their writing, but also to learn more about Hawai'ian culture by actually doing or participating in the things they were writing about.

Because the students got much of their material from real people, not books, some of the projects included in this book may not be completely authentic from an archeological or anthropological point of view. However, as a wise Hawai'i woman told our class, the Hawai'ian culture is a living culture that is evolving and changing. Some of the old methods of doing things have changed through time. Many of the projects and practices that we talk about in this book are still in use today, both by native Hawai'ians, and by the more recent immigrants to Hawai'i. And because Hawai'i is a living, fluid culture, there may be variations from person to person in how an item is made or a tradition is recorded which has worked its way into our presentations in this book.

The students used many sources to gather the information for their articles: interviews with local people, presentations to groups, classes, the local library, field trips, and some internet research (though that was discouraged). Another great resource was the many Hawai'ian cultural festivals offered by various state, national, and private parks that my students were able to attend.

When I envisioned this book, I had no idea how or where it would take us. Now that the project is over, I can see that it has given all of us a greater appreciation of the remarkable Hawai'ian culture. I am so proud of my students and what they have accomplished. I hope that this experience has been as wonderful for them as it has been for me.

Susan Kilbride, March 2013

Table of Contents

Uses of Hawai'ian Plants
by Dylan Kilbride

Most of the plants in this chapter are either native to the Hawai'ian islands or were brought there by the Hawai'ian people to use for food, medicine, house building, or other purposes. The plants in this chapter are just a fraction of all the plants that the early Hawai'ians used, but they are some of the most important.

Kalo, Taro, Colocasia esculenta

Kalo, more commonly known as taro, is one of the most important food crops that the Hawai'ians brought to the islands. It has large spade-shaped leaves that droop toward the ground. The stems grow out of a large corm—a bulbous formation made up of stem tissue. The corms can only be eaten after they are cooked; otherwise they are inedible due to the large amount of calcium oxalate they contain.

A Nene in a Taro Field on Kaua'i

There are two ways to grow taro, either in large flat fields that have been flooded with water or on dry land. In areas without wetlands only dry land taro can be grown. However, even taro planted on dry land needs up to sixty inches of rainfall to survive.

One of the major foods made from taro is called poi. To make poi, the early Hawai'ians placed taro corms on a board called a papa ku'i 'ai and mashed them with a pounding stone called a pōhaku ku'i 'ai.

First the corms were sliced with the side of the pounder, and the resulting chunks were slowly mashed down using a rolling motion. Then, a small amount of water was added to the board and the corms were mashed down even further until they became a thick paste. The term poi is actually a word for anything that is mashed in this fashion. Poi made from taro (kalo) is called poi kalo; poi made from ulu (breadfruit) is called poi ulu, and so on.

The early Hawai'ians also ate the taro leaves, which can be cooked and eaten like spinach. The leaves had to be handled carefully. They contain the same toxin as the corms, and if they are crushed, they will inject tiny needle-like crystals into the hand, which causes a rash. That is why it is so important to cook both the leaves and the corms thoroughly before eating them.

Taro Fields on Kaua'i

Naupaka kahakai, Scaevola taccada

This shrub with its pretty half flowers is a common sight around many Hawai'ian beaches. There is also a very different mountain variety, but still with the familiar half flower. The leaves of the coastal variety are thick, and the berries are small and green, or white.

The Half Flower of the Naupaka Kahakai

There were many Hawai'ian legends about this plant, mainly revolving around its flower. According to one version of the legend, there were two lovers, a commoner and a princess. It was forbidden for a commoner and a royal to marry, so when the gods found out about their love, the lovers were killed and turned into two half-flower plants. One was placed high in the mountains, and the other was placed on the shore so that they could never be together, and their flowers would never be whole.

The ancient Hawai'ians used this plant as famine food, because, though edible, the berries are small and bitter.

'Ākia, Wikstromia uva-ursi

This shrub was used as a fish toxin to stupefy fish in order to make them easier to catch. The leaves, bark, and berries were ground up and placed in fish ponds in baskets. The juice spread throughout the pond, stunning the fish and making them easier to catch. The poisoned fish did not hurt the people who ate them, but this method of fishing is now prohibited for the sake of the fish.

'Ākia Plant

Ulu, Breadfruit, Artocarpus altilis

Ulu is a large tree with broad, shiny leaves that branch out. The fruit is very bumpy and green. Ulu was one of the plants brought to the islands by the Hawai'ians in their canoes.

Ulu was a very important food source for the Hawai'ian people. It is very high in starch, and is sometimes considered a bread substitute. It was used in many different ways, but one popular dish was called piele 'ulu. This desert was made by mashing a breadfruit, then mixing in coconut cream until it was a thick paste. The paste was wrapped in ti leaves and baked in an imu (a cooking pit). The sap of the ulu was also used as chewing gum.

Ulu Tree

'Awapuhi, Shampoo Ginger
Zingiber zerumbet

'Awapuhi is a small ginger plant. It has large green flower heads with white flowers sticking out of the sides. The leaves are long and shiny green. The flower heads are saturated with a sudsy oil. In English it is called shampoo ginger because the oils from it are used in hair care products.

'Āwapuhi Flower Head

The Hawai'ians used shampoo ginger for curing various illnesses, including skin infections, cuts, headaches, and toothaches. It was also used as a flavoring, and the leaves were used to wrap fish or to flavor meats. The underground stems are very fragrant and were used for perfuming tapa cloth.

'Āwapuhi Leaves

'Aweoweo, Chenopodium oahuense

'Aweoweo is a small shrub with greenish-silver leaves and clusters of very small seeds. The leaves are shaped vaguely like spades and have a fishy smell when crushed. They were sometimes cooked and added to other dishes for their flavor. The wood was used to carve fishhooks.

'Aweoweo Plant

Pāpala-kēpua, Pisonia brunoniana

Pāpala-kēpua is a tropical forest plant with ovular shiny green leaves. It has white flowers with long green stalks. The seeds are black, about one and a half inches long, and extremely sticky.

The ancient Hawai'ians would harvest the seeds' sticky coating and rub it on branches below flowers that certain birds drank nectar

Pāpala-kēpua

from. The birds would land on the sticky coating and get stuck to the branch. The Hawai'ians then harvested their feathers for capes and other items.

The wood of pāpala-kēpua is fast burning. Sometimes dried branches were lit and thrown off cliffs, where they shot out sparks like firecrackers. People would gather below the cliffs in canoes to watch the show.

Sticky Pāpala-kēpua Seeds

'Iliahi, Sandalwood, Santalum paniculatum

This native tree can mostly be found in deep valleys and other remote areas. The leaves are light green, and the seeds are green or purple. The small flowers are gold with four triangular-shaped petals. The trees can be up to thirty feet high. The roots are parasitic, feeding off the roots of other plants. The flowers and heartwood were used for scenting kapa cloth and coconut oil.

Sandalwood trees were very popular for their scent. In fact, one might say that they were overly popular. Millions of pounds of Hawai'ian sandalwood were chopped down and shipped around the world. Now there are very few sandalwood trees left on Hawai'i.

Sandalwood Flowers

'Awa, Kava, Piper methysticum

'Awa is a shrub with spade-like leaves. It was mainly used as a narcotic. A drink made from its roots was used before battles, as it was thought to increase the senses and dull pain. It was also used for healing purposes. This drink, more commonly called kava, was made by pounding up the mature root with water. However, it is not at all appetizing, and the brownish drink tastes like mud.

'Awa roots were also pounded into animal livers and dropped into the ocean to catch sharks. The sharks would eat the liver and became stupefied. Then a noose was slipped over their heads and they were dragged to shore.

Awa Leaves

Hāpu'u, Hawai'ian Tree Fern, Cibotium glaucoma

This large native fern is found in forested areas. It is best identified by the soft brown clumps of down that cling to the bases of its stems and sprouts.

The downy fibers, known as pula, were scorched and placed on tired and aching muscles—as a sort of heating pad. They were also soaked with other medicines and placed on cuts. The inner bark of this fern was mixed with other ingredients and used as a medicine to clean the blood.

Hāpu'u Down

Hāpu'u Leaves

Hala, Screw Pine, Pandanus tectorius

Hala is a large tree with aerial roots like a mangrove. And like a mangrove, it can survive in coastal areas. The leaves are long and have sharp spines. The fruits are green and are vaguely shaped like pineapples, only they hang from the leaf clusters. The branches are brown and smooth, and the ground beneath these trees is almost always littered with dead leaves and seeds.

The Hawai'ians used the seeds of these trees as brushes for painting kapa cloth, as the tips are frayed like brushes.

The leaves from the hala were woven into jewelry and mats. The Hawai'ians also used the mats for sails for their boats. The fruits are edible, though mealy.

A Hala Nut

Hala Fruit

Koa, Acacia koi

Koa trees can be very tall and have curved leaves. The flowers are light, puffy, and yellow.

Among other things, koa wood was used for making canoes. Canoe makers had to be very careful which koa to cut down for a canoe. They would observe their chosen tree, and if a bird pecked on the tree, it meant that the tree had insects in it and was unusable. (Certain birds eat insects out of wood.) If the bird landed on the tree but did not peck, the tree could then be cut down. Koa bark was also used to make red dye.

Koa Leaves

Pua Kala, Hawai'ian Poppy, Agrimony glance

This white poppy has spiny leaves and stems. The yellow sap from the stem was applied to warts, and the root was chewed on to relieve toothaches.

Pili, Twisted Beardgrass, Heteropogon contortus

Pili grass was used to stuff mattresses and was burned for scent. The blades were used for black dye. Pili was also used for thatching. It is best identified by the twisted bunches that hold the blades together. These are its seeds. If you look carefully, you can see the small seeds at the end of the bunches.

Pili Seeds

Pili

Kukui, Candlenut Tree, Aleurites moluccana

The leaves of this tree are silvery and light green, and the flowers are small and white. The nuts are small, greenish brown, and sprout year round.

Pig carvings made from kukui wood were used to mark boundaries, and the inner bark was used to make a brownish red dye. But the part of the tree that was the most useful was the nuts. Their husks were used to make a grey dye, they were burned to make charcoal, they were strung into leis, they were roasted and mashed with seasoning to make a popular flavoring (however, the nut is also a powerful laxative, so only a small amount could be eaten at a time), and their oil was extracted for polishing wood or burning in lamps. Often many of them were skewered on a stick and lit to produce light. The following chapter has more information on kukui nuts and their oil.

Kukui Nut

Kukui Nut Tree

Olena, Turmeric, Curcuma longa

The root of this broadleaved ginger was used as seasoning and also to dye kapa cloth. This plant is seasonal, lying dormant in the winter months. It was also an ingredient in a perfume dye worn by chiefs.

Olena Leaves

Hau, Hibiscus tiliaceus

This large shrub is found in coastal areas. The red and yellow flowers have five petals. The Hawai'ians made practice spears out of the wood, because it was very light. It was also a popular plant for making cordage. The inner bark of the tree was soaked in water for two weeks or more (with frequent changes of the water to keep it fresh), until the outer bark separated from the soft inner bark. The inner bark was then dried and the strands were twisted together to make a strong twine.

Hau

Hau bark before it has been separated

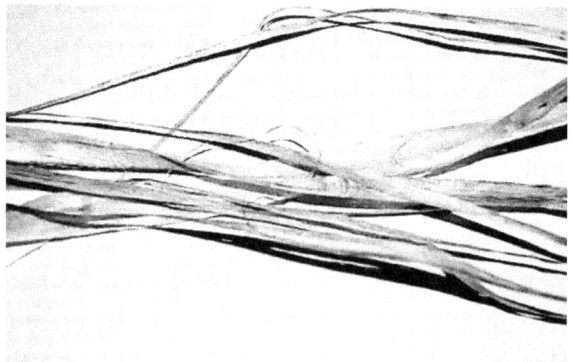

The inner bark after it has been peeled and dried

Cordage made from Hau

Kamani, Alexandrian laurel, Calophyllum inophyllum

This tree is a popular landscape tree. It has broad shiny leaves and large green nuts. These nuts were often hollowed out to make whistles. Kamani was a popular wood for carving. The sap, which smells like maple syrup, was used to treat stomach ulcers. The orange-smelling white flowers were used as perfume.

Kamani

The early Hawai'ians were very attuned to their environment and found uses for many of the plants that surrounded them. People today look at plants and see beautiful trees and bushes, but when the early Hawai'ians looked at them, they saw their supermarkets and drug stores.

Kukui Nut Oil
By Molly Russell

Common Name: Candlenut
Scientific Name: Aleurites moluccana
Hawai'ian Meaning: Light

The Polynesians who came to Hawai'i in their outrigger canoes were very careful planners. They brought along not only food for the trip, but seeds, plant cuttings, and supplies so that they could survive until their plants started to grow. Kukui nut trees were one of the many plants that they brought with them to Hawai'i. They used almost every part of the tree from roots to seeds. The tree served a range of purposes, such as fuel for light, medicinal remedies, dyes for tattoos and cloth, and fishing supplies.

The kukui nut tree also had a role in Hawai'ian mythology. The early Hawai'ians believed that the tree was a kinolau (a physical form of a Hawai'ian god) of the rainforest god Kama-pua'a. He was also known as the spirit of rain and growing things. Scattered throughout Hawai'ian mythology, Kamapu-a'a is seen annoying and trying to win the attention of the volcano goddess, Pele. Kamapua'a always liked damp, rainy valleys, and this is where you can find kukui nut trees grow-ing to this day.

Another belief of the ancient Hawai'ians was that if you threw a kukui nut into a fire, you could put a curse on a thief. Usually a Hawai'ian priest would throw three nuts into the fire. Each time he threw one in, he would ask the thief to ad-mit his wrongdoings. If the thief didn't answer by the third nut, the priest would put a curse of punishment on the criminal. The thief believed that punishment would come from the gods. The guilt and fear that he felt was part of the punishment.

The kukui nut tree has silver green leaves about eight inches across that are similar in shape to maple tree leaves. The young leaves have a white fuzz on them that shines in the sun. The white flowers are about one centimeter across and bloom in clusters that usually appear on the tips of its branches. The nuts are green and are about two inches across. They have a husk on the outside with a shell and a kernel on the inside. The trees can grow up to three feet in diameter and sixty feet tall.

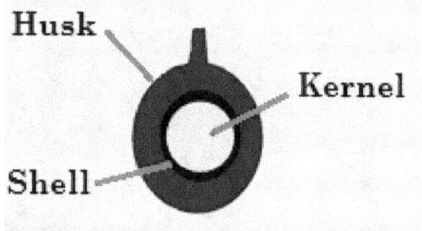

One common use of the kukui nut was for its oil. The nuts are eighty percent oil and are very flammable, providing light when burned. The oil was used as fuel in different types of lamps. One lamp, called a kalikukui, used kukui nuts strung on a coconut leaf midrib. The top nut was set on fire and burned for about three minutes. As it burned out, the next nut in line caught fire, and the burned-out kukui nut was broken off. It was the children's job to make sure the new nut always caught fire and to replace the lamp when it burned out.

Another type of lamp was an oil lamp. The Hawai'ians would take a stone bowl, fill it with kukui nut oil, and insert a wick. For more light they would put in more wicks. This type of lamp was called a poho kukui.

Aside from light, the oil was also used for protecting wood; staining surfboards; stimulating hair growth; preventing stretch marks; and curing stomach aches, abdominal problems, burns, and headaches. Today kukui nut oil is also found helpful in treating infection, fungus, fatigue, and constipation. Its most common use today is as a moisturizer. It contains antioxidant vitamins A, C, and E and can be used to protect skin from sun, wind and salt.

Fun Facts

In the early 1800s, 10,000 barrels of kukui nut oil per year were shipped to Alaska.

Today kukui nut oil is used in race cars.

Kukui is the state tree of Hawai'i.

Making Kukui Nut Oil

Many people today still make their own kukui nut oil, and you can too if you follow these instructions.

The first thing to do is to collect several dozen kukui nuts off the ground from around a kukui nut tree. Nuts that have fallen off the tree are usually ripe and easier to crack. However, the really old ones can be rotten and smell awful. Use your nose to try to pick the best ones. Once you have collected your nuts, remove their husks and place them in a bucket of water. Throw out the floating nuts and save the nuts that sink to the bottom.

Take the nuts that you saved, and crack the shells off them with a hammer. You should wear safety glasses when you do this.

Next, take the kernels and place them on a baking sheet. Bake them in an oven for fifteen minutes at 450 degrees.

After they have cooled, use a rolling pin to crush the nuts into tiny, fine chunks.

Now, place the ground kernels in a glass jar with a lid, and place it so that it is sitting in sunlight:

Over the next few weeks, the oil will slowly rise to the top of the jar. Continue to add more roasted nuts and pour off the oil as desired. Add five drops of grapefruit seed extract and two drops of vitamin E oil per ounce of kukui nut oil to help preserve it. Kukui nut oil can go rancid very quickly.

How to Make a Kalikukui Lamp

To make a kalikukui lamp, you will first need to collect three to five kukui nuts. You may want to collect some extras in case some of them crack. Select them in the same way that you selected the nuts for making kukui nut oil: pick the ripe nuts from the ground, husk them, and soak them in water to pick the nuts that sink.

Next, put the nuts in the oven with their shells on for fifteen minutes at 450 degrees.

Once you have placed the nuts in the oven, do not open your oven until after the nuts have cooled for an hour! This is very important because the nuts can explode!

There is an old Hawai'ian story about someone who lost an eye by roasting kukui nuts on a fire, so do not open your oven until the nuts are completely cool.

When nuts are baked and cooled, crack off the shells from the kernel. Be careful to keep the kernels whole. Thread the kernels on a coconut leaf midrib. The nuts will be soft, so they will thread easily. A bamboo skewer can be used in place of a coconut midrib.

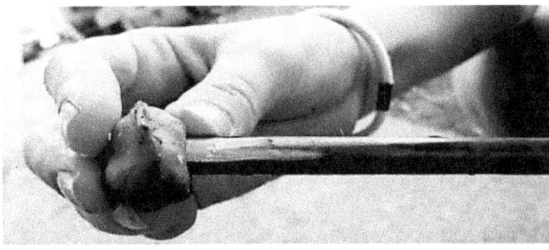
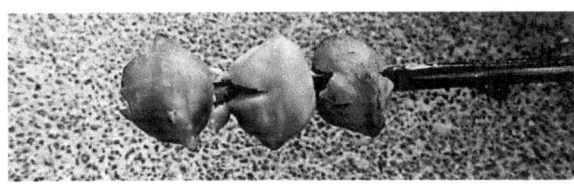

Stick the lamp into the ground or lean it up against a stone. Whatever you do, make sure that there is nothing flammable nearby that could catch on fire. You should also have some water handy in case you need to put your lamp out quickly. Light the top kernel. When the top kernel goes out, break it off and make sure that the next nut in line is lit. Each nut will burn for about three minutes.

Hawai'ian Palm Frond Crafts
By Emily Risley

The coconut palm was an important part of ancient Hawai'ian life. The nut was used for food and utensils, and the frond was used for roofing, mats, tools, baskets, needles, and toys. One of these toys was the palm frond fish.

Making a Palm Frond Fish

Materials

To make a palm frond fish, all you need is one coconut palm frond leaflet per fish:

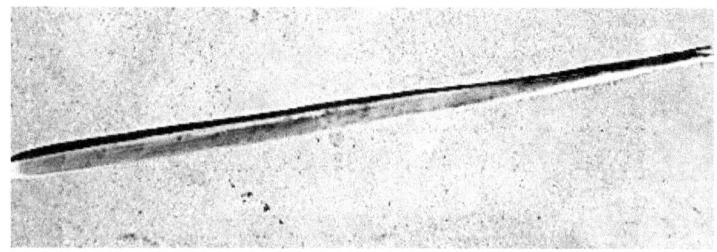

Other types of palms will work as well, but the best sized, shaped, and most durable frond for this project is the coconut palm.

You will also need a pair of scissors.

Making your Fish

To begin, rip or cut off one palm frond leaflet. If you have small hands, use one of the skinnier leaflets found on the end of the frond.

Next, take the scissors and cut off the base of the leaflet. Then cut the leaflet along both sides of the midrib. You can discard the base and midrib:

Now grasp one of the half-leaflets, or leaflet 1, between your pinky and the rest of your fingers. Leave about an inch coming out the back. If you are right handed, do this in your left hand, and vice-versa:

In your free hand, take the longer part of leaflet 1 and wrap it upwards, coming down the other side and back out towards you between your pinky and your third finger. Repeat this once more:

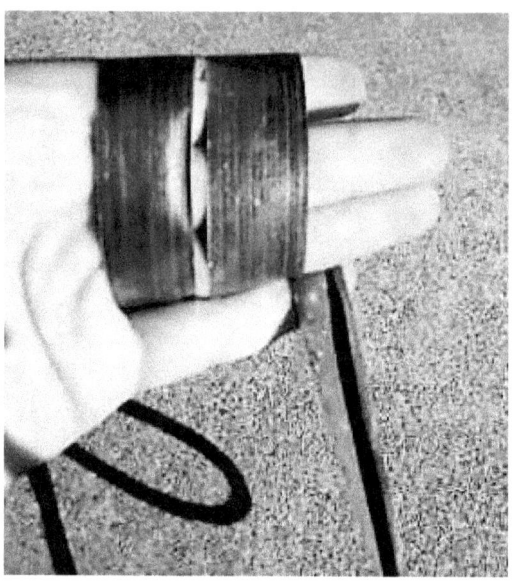

Next, grab the other half-leaflet, or leaflet 2, with your free hand, keeping leaflet 1 firmly in place with the other. Tuck about two inches of the cut end of leaflet 2 under the wrap farthest from your fingertips:

Bring the long end of leaflet 2 around to the *back* of your hand, between your index and middle fingers. Tuck leaflet 2 under the wrap closest to your fingertips, and over the other wrap:

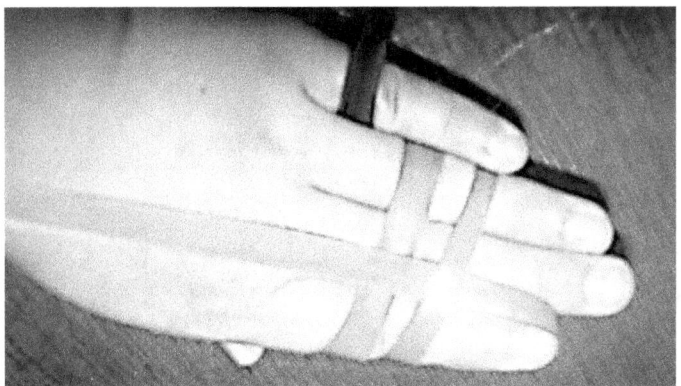

Next, turn your palm up, take leaflet 2 and bring it over your fingers and under your thumb. Then bring it under the "tail" at the top, over the wrap farthest from your fingertips, and under the wrap closest to your fingertips:

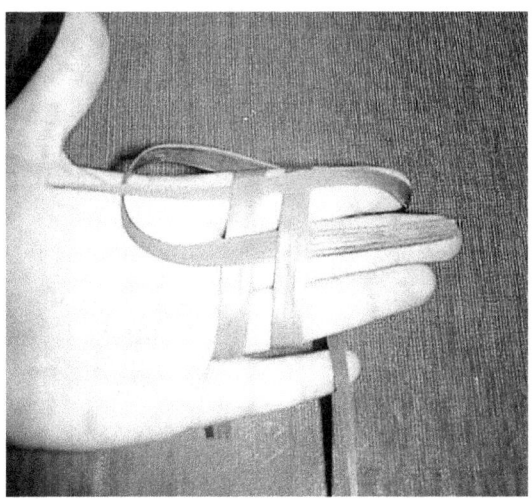

Pull leaflet 2 tight, so that the loop in the previous photo is tight against the wraps.

Now things get tricky, so keep a tight clamp on leaflet 1. Turn your hand over and slip leaflet 2 over the tip of your ring finger, then over the wrap closest to your fingertips, and under the wrap farthest from your fingertips. Be careful here, it is easy to slip it under the wrong wrap:

Next, carefully slide the whole thing off your fingers. Pull on each of the ends until it resembles a fish. Even if you think something went wrong with it, keep pulling, because often it just looks that way.

Finally, take the scissors and trim the leaves down. If you leave the top fin of the fish longer, you can tie it to something. To make a simple ornament, tie the top fin to a string.

Now you've made a palm frond fish. You can use it for many things such as decorating, as a gift, or you can fill the pocket inside the body of the fish with something nice smelling and use it as an air freshener. You could also use it in the next project.

Making a Palm Frond Fishing Rod

Materials

Since the early Hawai'ians did not use fishing rods, this toy project was probably developed in more modern times.

To make a palm frond fishing rod, you will need one large palm frond leaflet. (Though you might want to have more than one on hand, in case of mistakes.) You will also need a palm frond fish and a pair of scissors.

Making Your Palm Frond Fishing Rod

First trim off the bottom end of the palm frond leaf. Next, take the scissors and separate (but don't detach completely) the sides of the leaf from the midrib. Begin at the tip (you can cut off the tip if it helps) and skim the scissors down each side of the midrib stopping before the last three to five inches. Then, cut the tip ends of the leaflet halves off as shown in the diagram below:

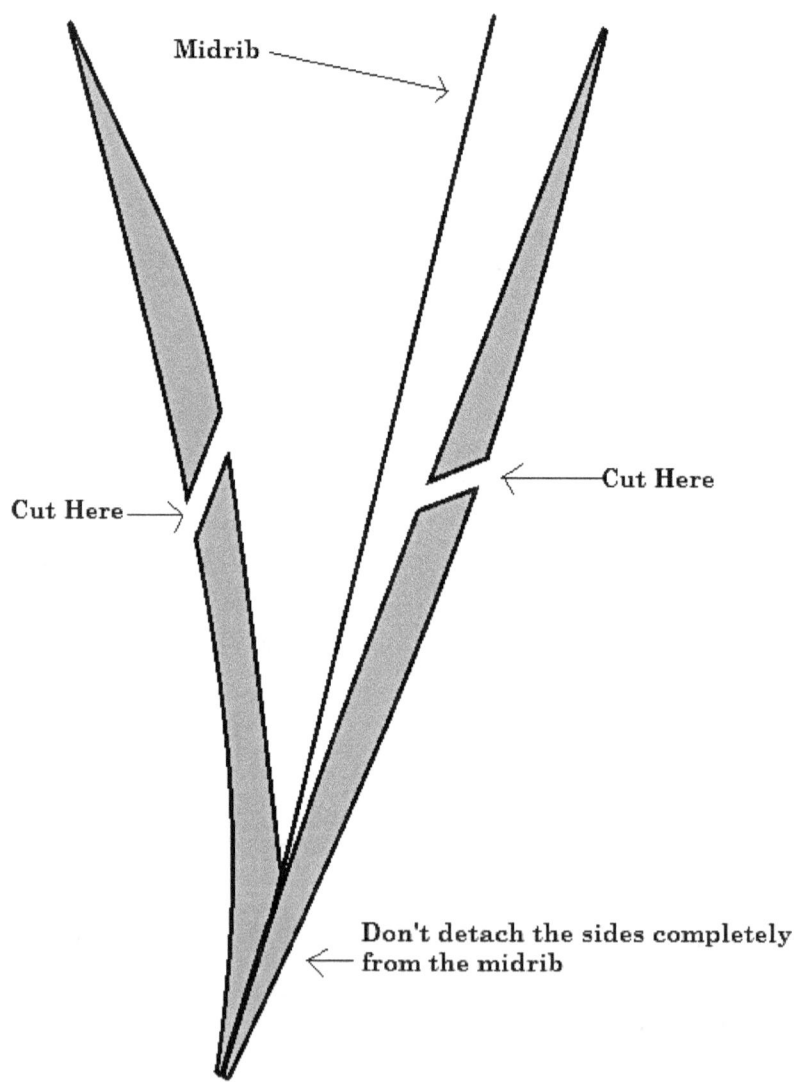

Next lay the leaflet out in front of you, with the base towards you. The sides should be placed so that the midrib is to your left, and the leaflets to your right. Lay the leaf flat, so the two halves are on top of each other.

Take the top half-leaflet, or leaflet A, and fold it to your right. You'll want it to fold it *under* the midrib:

Now take the bottom half-leaflet, or leaflet B, and fold it over leaflet A, this time on *top* of the midrib:

Take leaflet B, the one that's on top now, and fold it upwards. Leaflet B should now run parallel to the midrib, on the left side. Throughout the project, remember when folding the leaflets up, to fold the leaflets as close to the midrib as possible, but not over it:

Now, take leaflet A, and fold it upwards as well, on top of leaflet B. Remember to fold the leaflet close to the midrib:

Leaflet A is now on top. Keep hold of it and fold it to your right. Fold it under the midrib, and out to the side:

Next, take leaflet B and fold it on top of leaflet A, except this time go on top of the midrib:

Now, fold leaflet B (the leaf on top this time) upwards, so that it is parallel to the midrib:

Next, fold leaflet A over leaflet B:

Leaflet A is now on top. Fold it to your left, tucking it under the midrib:

By now you should be getting a feel for the pattern. Next fold leaflet B over leaflet A:

Continue with this pattern until you only have a 1 ½ inches of leaf left. You'll want to end with one leaflet heading either to the left or right, and the other one heading upwards:

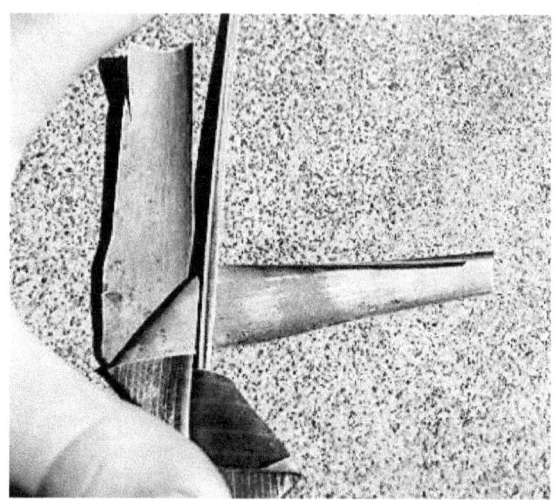

To finish your fishing rod, trim your leaflets so that you have pointed ends on both leaflets A and B:

Finally, tie the two tips together in a simple knot:

Now you're ready to add the fish to the fishing rod. First, thread the midrib of the top of the rod through the front loop of the fish:

Now bring the tip of the midrib back around to the rest of the stem and tie it in a simple knot. There is no need to tie it too tight; it usually sticks pretty well:

Your completed fishing rod should look something like this:

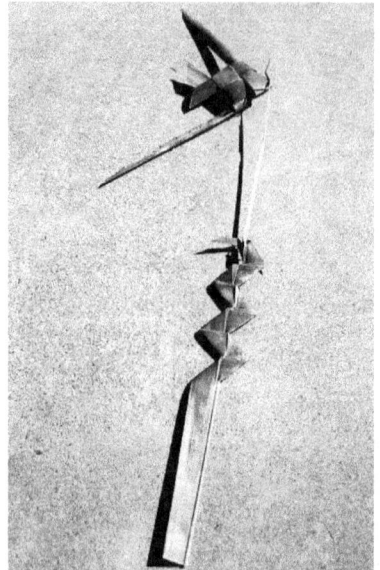

Hawai'ian Feather Work
By Molly Russell

The Polynesians who came to Hawai'i brought with them the craft of working with feathers. Later Hawai'ians, using endemic birds and plants, perfected the art, and Hawai'ian feather work today is considered some of the most advanced in the world.

Traditionally, feather work was only worn by high ranking royalty and priests. The Hawai'ians believed birds had spiritual power and that feathers carried their magic properties such as keen eyes, speed, and endurance. It was illegal for common people to collect or wear them. Feathers were used to make various items worn and used by royalty.

The ahu'ula, or feather cape, was a symbol of power and rank for the ali'i (chiefs and nobility). Different designs in the capes showed rank and status, and the length of the cape also showed rank. King Kamehameha's long cape was made entirely of over 450,000 yellow feathers of the rare Mamo bird. It took 60,000 birds to make the cape. The use of yellow and no other color in his cape showed that he was so powerful that he did not need any designs on his cape like other chiefs to show his power and rank.

Feather Cape from the King Kamehameha Hotel in Kona, HI

Kahili were tall feather staffs that were sometimes as much as thirty feet long. They were carried by guards for the chiefs. Smaller kahili called kahili lele were held by chiefs and used to ward off bad spirits. The next chapter in this book has directions on how to make a kahili lele.

Lei hulu were feather leis

worn by both men and women. There were two different traditional types of lei hulu. The lei poepoe was made from crimped feathers and worn around the neck. The crimping made the feathers stand out more. A lei kamoe was worn on the head or neck. Feathers in a lei kamoe were tied more thickly and not crimped, so they lay flat along the lei. The center cord around which the feathers were tied was made of plant fibers.

'Uli'uli were feathered gourd rattles used for hula.

Feather gathering was an important job, and the feather gatherers were called po'e hahai manu. One method they used to collect feathers was called kahekahe. This method took advantage of the fact

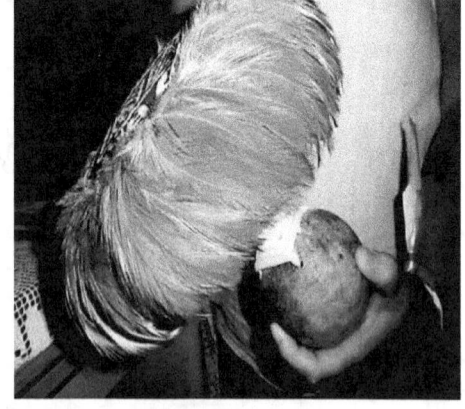

Uli'uli

that many Hawai'ian birds like nectar from the 'ohi'a tree. In this technique most of the flowers were cut from an 'ohi'a tree. Then, breadfruit sap was put on the branches with the remaining flowers. The birds that landed on the branches would get stuck in the sap, allowing the feather gatherers to catch the birds. After a few feathers were plucked from each bird, salve was applied to help the birds heal, the sticky sap was removed from their feet, and they were released to grow new feathers. This was done during the time when the birds molt so the feathers were easy to remove.

MAMO

Hawai'ian feather work would not have been possible without the beautiful endemic birds of Hawai'i. The yellow wing, neck, and tail feathers of the black Mamo and O'o birds were very rare. Only a few feathers could be gathered from each bird. The yellow feathers were the most valuable and could only be worn by those of highest rank. Polynesians valued red above all colors, but when they moved to Hawai'i, yellow feathers became more prized because they were harder to find in Hawai'i. Green feathers came from the 'Akialoa and red feathers from the I'iwi and 'Apapane. These birds

Ō'ō

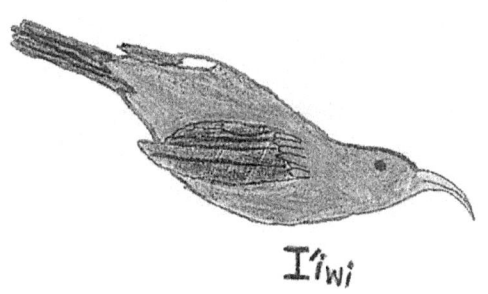

I'iwi

were more plentiful and often they were killed and eaten. Later, King Kamehameha prohibited the bird catchers from killing them so that the birds would still be there for his children to see. Traditional colors for Hawai'ian feather work were red, yellow, black, and sometimes green.

After collecting enough feathers, the ancient Hawai'ians would tie small bundles of a few feathers together and then tie each bundle to a netting to create a cape. For the feather helmets worn by royalty, a frame was made of plant fibers and then netting was stretched over it to tie on the feathers.

Feathers Being Tied to a Modern-Day Netting

A Feather Helmet from the King Kamehameha Hotel in Kona, HI

Netting and string used for tying was often made from the olonā plant. Fiber from olonā was prized for the strong cords that could be made from it.

The art of Hawai'ian feather work is still practiced today. Creating traditional feather work pieces helps people learn about ancient Hawai'ian traditions and culture. Today, Hawai'ian feather work is not just for royalty but can be worn and enjoyed by anyone. Feather working has changed over the centuries but in many ways it is still the same.

One big difference is that many Hawai'ian endemic birds are now endangered or extinct. In place of their feathers, goose feathers are dyed so they look like traditional Hawai'ian bird feathers. Other feathers such as turkey, peacock and pheasant are also used for their natural patterns. This has allowed many more patterns and colors to come into modern feather work.

Another big difference today is in lei feather work. In the 1820s, missionaries brought metal needles and cotton thread to the islands. The humu papa is a lei made by using a needle and thread to sew feathers onto a piece of fabric or felt.

To create a humu papa, feathers are sewn onto a felt backing. Careful selection of the feathers is made based on their size, shape, and color. The preparation of the feathers can take more time than the sewing.

A mirror is placed under the lei while sewing to make sure the stitches don't show on the back side of the lei. The feathers should overhang one quarter inch over the felt backing. This is done by careful selection, measurement and placement of the feathers. It is also important not to sew the feathers on too tight so they don't pucker. Each feather is sewn onto the felt with four stitches. The feathers are layered with two to

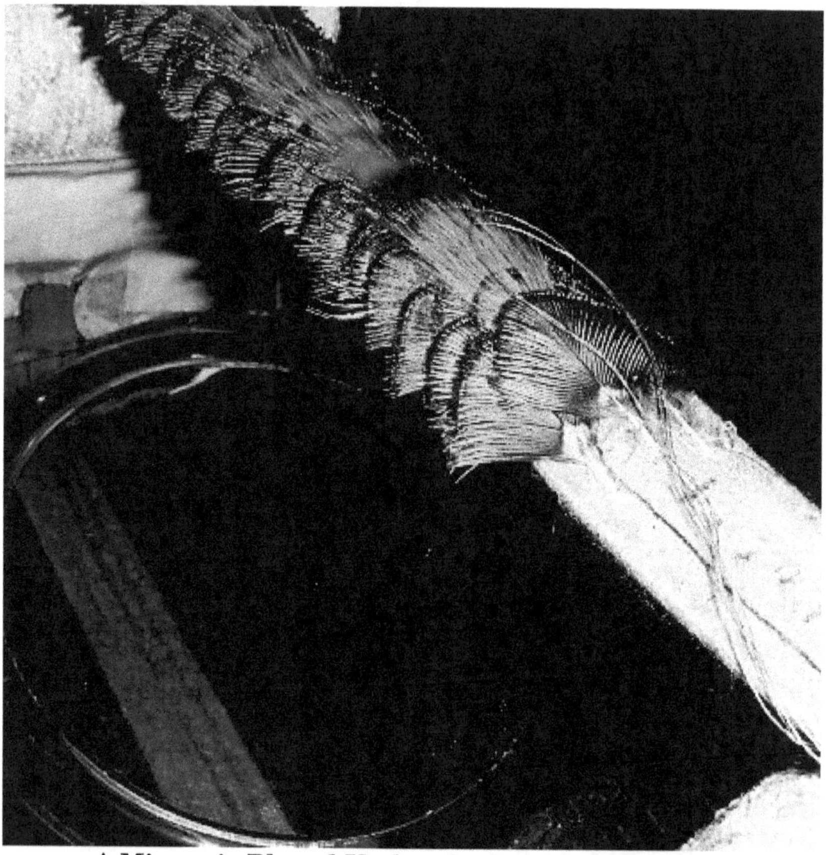

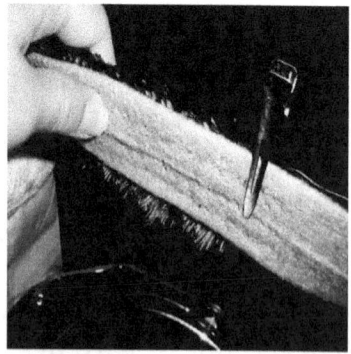

A Mirror is Placed Under the Lei while Sewing

three feathers in each layer. The distance between rows of feathers can be as small as one sixteenth of an inch. The goal of most feather workers is to make the flat lei feel and look like the feathers on a bird's breast. The felt is marked where each row will go. Each feather is held in place with a clip while being sewn.

The back side of a finished humu papa shows only small dents where the stitches are. Some feather workers trim the feathers along the sides when they are finished to make it even around the edges, but the best way to do it is to sew the feathers on correctly from the beginning. Humu papa are made to be worn as hatbands and they are measured and made to fit only a specific hat.

The Back Side of a Humu Papa

How to Make a Feather Flower

One of the first projects a beginning feather worker learns is how to make feather flowers.

Tools and Supplies

Six inches of floral wire
Green floral tape
Stamens
Needle-nosed pliers
Scissors
Ruler
Shuttle to put thread on for easy tying
Ten Feathers of any color (5 each of 2 colors works nicely)
A few extra feathers (just in case)
Polyester thread–it is helpful for beginners if the thread is a
contrasting color to the feathers.

Use the pliers to make a small hook on one end of the floral wire. Take three stamens and put them halfway through
the hook and bend them up in half so they are pointing up.
Bend the hook closed tight around stamens:

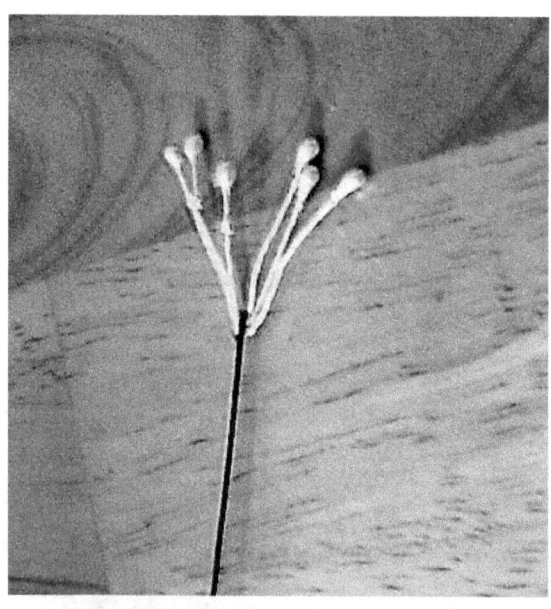

Next, start at the hook, and cover the wire with green floral tape:

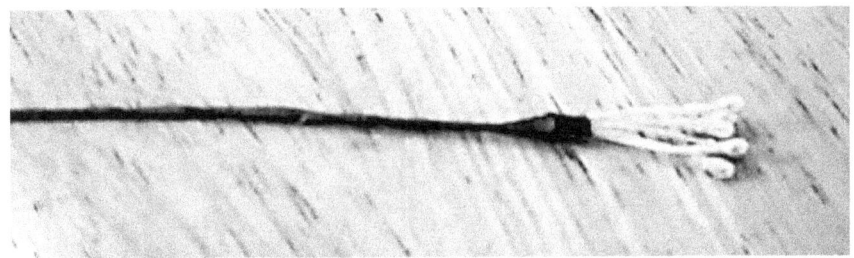

Now, select ten feathers that are full and long:

One at a time, take the feathers and measure two inches from the *tip* down and cut them:

Crimp each feather one quarter inch from the quill end so that if you hold the feather part, the quill bends down:

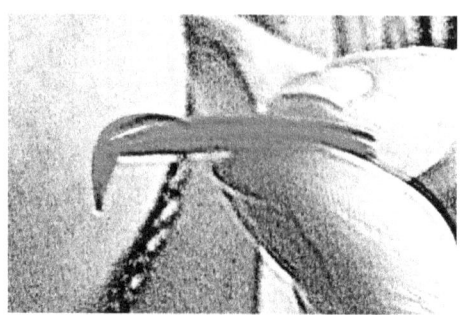

Tie the quill end of the first feather on to the wire with two wraps around of thread in a clockwise direction. Tie a half hitch knot to hold it secure:

Tie on the second feather right next to the first using the same method:

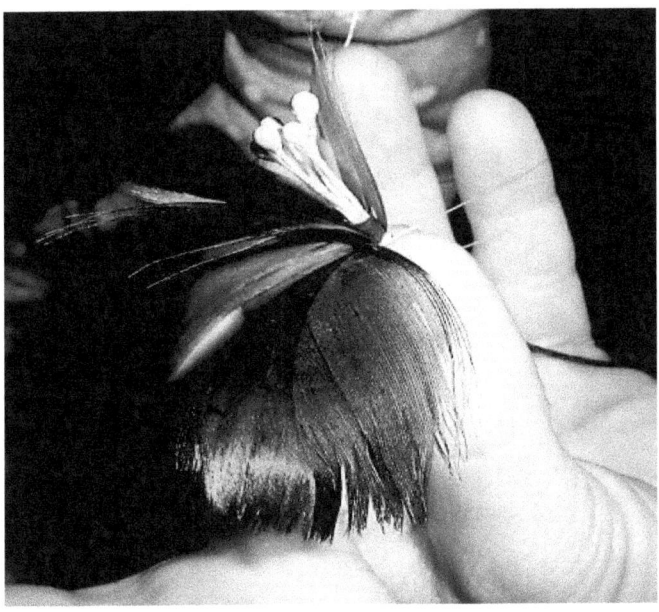

Keep adding feathers around the wire until all the feathers are fastened on to your liking. After all the feathers are secure they can be wiggled around for better placement if needed. Tie off the thread with two more half-hitch knots:

Finally, wrap floral tape over the thread and keep going down until you reach the bottom of the wire:

Twist the flowers into your hair or hat and enjoy!

Hawai'ian feather work was very important to the ancient Hawai'ians because they believed the birds had strong spiritual powers. Today, when people learn the art of feather work they also get to learn about the importance of the birds and feathers to the early Hawai'ians. Although the styles of feather work have changed throughout the years, it still contains much of what is special in feather work. Unlike in ancient Hawai'i, however, today anyone can learn to do feather work from classes and books.

How to Make a Kahili Lele
By Pearl Dickson

A kahili is a staff topped with feathers that was a sign of royalty for the Hawai'ian chiefs (ali'i). Kahili varied in length from two to thirty feet tall. The attendants who carried them had to make sure the feathers didn't touch the ground, as that was considered disrespectful. Feathers were very precious to the ancient Hawai'ians. They were like gold or jewels, and were difficult to obtain, which is one reason why kahili were a symbol of the ali'i. Smaller kahili called kahili lele were used to ward off bad spirits.

Steps to Make a Kahili Lele

To make a kahili lele, you will need a stick, some tape, and feathers. Kahili lele were often made with feathers from the Koae, Nene, Iiwi, 'O'o, Owl, Frigate bird, or even chickens.

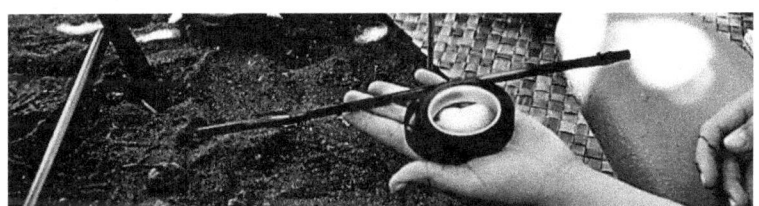

1) Take your tape and wind it around the top of your stick three to four times:

2) Next, place a feather in between the tape and the stick and wrap the tape around the stick two more times to hold the feather in place. Put another feather next to it and hold it in place with two more wraps of the tape. Keep doing this until you have a ring of feathers around the stick. As you do this, make sure that your feathers are always facing out. They should look something like this:

3) The quill ends of your feathers should be covered with the tape. Put the next round of feathers down a little farther down on the stick and repeat the same process.

4) You can make your kahili lele as long or as short as you want by adding rings of feathers.

A Completed Kahili Lele

Hula
By Teah Van Bergen

Hula is an ancient Hawai'ian dance that has been around for hundreds of years. In the past it was used to worship the Hawai'ian gods. The Polynesians who came to Hawai'i in their canoes brought their style of dance to the islands, and hula developed from those early dances. Hula was, and still is, used to portray olis (chants), and meles (songs). Hula describes these chants and songs with motions and that can be either fast or slow. The instruments used for making a beat to dance hula to are the ipu heke 'ole, 'ili'ili, 'uli'uli, kala'au, and pu'ili.

Ipu heke 'ole

The ipu heke 'ole is a drum made from a gourd. It is used to make a deep rhythm. This is done by patting the sides or bottom. The following chapter tells how to make an ipu heke 'ole.

Pu'ili

Pu'ili are bamboo sticks with slits cut in the top that are used to make a rattling sound. This is

'Uli'uli

done by hitting the tops of the sticks together. Kala'au are wooden sticks that are hit together to make a rhythm, and 'ili'ilis are stones that are clapped together. 'Uli'ulis are feathered shakers.

Hula was, and still is, a passionate dance. Anyone (male or female) can dance the hula. There are two different kinds of hula—auana and kahiko. Kahiko is old, traditional hula while auana is a more modern and graceful form of hula. Kahiko uses quick, short movements and is faster than auana. Some sources say that originally only men were allowed to dance the hula, so kahiko is more of a masculine hula. However, the journals from Captain Cook's voyages mention seeing women dance also. Today both men and women practice and perform kahiko.

Below there are some photos of the different styles of clothing used in kahiko and auana. Auana developed after western contact, and the instruments used for auana are more western based, such as the guitar, ukulele, and double bass.

A Dress for Auana   **A Dress for Kahiko**

Hula dancers often use various types of leis as accessories. They use wristlets, anklets, and head leis. The leis can be made of flowers such as red and yellow lehus, puakeni'keni, and plumeria. Shells and nuts were also used for leis.

Hula was used to praise the goddess of the volcano, Pele. Legend has it that Hi'iaka, Pele's sister, danced hula to her, and so dancing hula to Pele became a tradition. But, the owner of the dance was a goddess named Laka, who was often given offerings by hula dancers.

Hula was performed at regular daily events and for entertainment. It served as entertainment for chiefs at special events as well. Hula performances were a form of loyalty and flattery to the chief. The males would often start the performance and the females would close the event or ceremony.

The missionaries who came to Hawai'i disproved of hula, so when Queen Ka'ahumanu became a Christian, she banned hula and took down all of the statues of the Hawai'ian gods. Queen Ka'ahumanu was accepted into the church in 1825 and in 1830 she announced that public performances of hula were illegal. Because of this, hula was only danced in secret for decades. Then, King Kalakaua (king of Hawai'i from 1874-1891) declared that "Hula is the language of the heart and therefore the heartbeat of the Hawaiian people." Decades later, the modern Merry Monarch hula festival was named in his honor. People from all around the world come to watch and preform in it.

With the end of the monarchy, many things changed about the Hawai'ian culture. Hula lost its purpose, and served mainly as entertainment for tourists. Many of Hawai'i's cultural activities lost their meaning, until 1970, when there was a revival of the Hawai'ian culture.

Halaus are groups of hula dancers who practice and perform together. Each halau has a kumu hula, who is the leader/teacher of the halau. It is considered offensive to switch to another halau. Dancers are very loyal to their halaus and do not switch very often.

Every movement in hula has an exact meaning, and every movement by the dancer has great significance. Hand movements are coupled with foot movements. The movements of a dancer's body might represent certain plants, animals, or even war. For example, in imitating a shark or a waving palm tree, the hula dancer may actually pretend to be that organism.

There are two main positions in hula: noho (to sit) and luna (to stand). Some dances utilize both forms. Many dancers also chant while dancing.

Noho   **Luna**

Hula is a hard and inspiring Hawai'ian activity that everyone is capable of learning. The strength and determination that is shown in this dance is empowering. Hula requires skill and adaptation. From graceful hand motions to strict and firm motions, hula demonstrates it all. Hula can bring out a fierce but graceful side of you that you may not have known of. Hula can reflect or pertain to different parts of you and your life.

Some Hula Dance Movements

Hela: Point your right toe forward, then pull your foot back. Do the same with the left foot and repeat these motions.

Ka'o: Move your right foot to the right, then follow with your left foot. Next do the same motion, this time starting with your left foot. Repeat.

Kaholo: Take four steps to the right and position your arms as shown above. Then switch to your left and take four steps to the left while changing the direction of your arms. Do this repeatedly.

Uehe: Lightly stomp on the ground. Then lift and widen your legs as shown. Do the same with the other foot and repeat.

Making an Ipu Heke 'Ole
(Gourd Drum)
By Charlee Brown

The Polynesian colonists of Hawai'i brought with them many seeds and plants. One of the most important of these was the ipu (gourd). An ipu is an amazing fruit. When it is immature it is green, but as it dries out it turns brown and gets harder and harder, until it finally has a wood-like texture. Ipus were used for medicine, bowls, water containers, and musical instruments. One of these instruments is the ipu heke 'ole or the single-gourd drum.

An Immature Ipu

Things You Need to Make an Ipu Heke 'Ole

*A ripe ipu
*String or twine
*A saw
*A drill

*Coconut Husk
*Oil for polish
*Sand (preferably at a beach)

Steps to Make an Ipu Heke 'Ole

1. First, you'll need to obtain a dried ipu. You can grow them or buy them. The outer skin should be hard and look like wood.

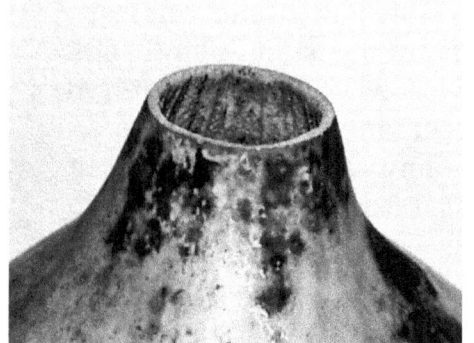

2. After you have picked out your ipu, you need to cut the top off with a saw. The size of the hole in the top will depend on where on the neck of the ipu you cut it.

3. Once you have picked out your ipu and have cut the top off, you need to scrub out all of the dust and dead pieces inside of it. The best place to do this is at the beach. Put sand and water in the ipu and shake it around. Keep doing this until it feels empty inside. Do not use a stick to clean it out, or you might accidentally poke a hole in it. Once the ipu is clean, rinse it out with water.

4. Using a drill, make a small hole on the side of the ipu, near the top. Be careful that you don't crack it—it is very delicate.

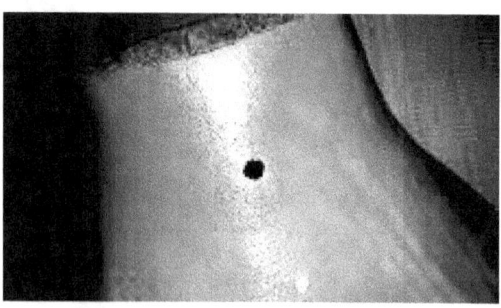

5. Now take a slice of coconut husk and scrape the outside of the ipu, rubbing away all the "rubbish." Do this until it feels like nothing else can come off of the ipu.

An Ipu Before it is Cleaned

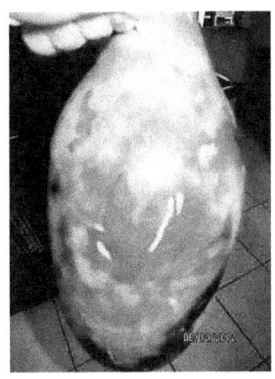

An Ipu After It Is Cleaned

6. Once you have cleaned off the outside of your ipu, take a piece of string or twine and put it through the small hole at the top. Tie it together in a loop. This string goes around your wrist while you play so that you don't drop the drum while you are playing it.

7. After you have made your drum, you can oil it. Pretty much, any oil will work, although coconut oil and kukui nut oil are the best. You should oil your ipu heke ʻole every two to three weeks to bring out the color and keep it from drying out.

A Finished Ipu Heke ʻOle

How to Dye an Ipu

by Charlee Brown

The people of the island of Ni'ihau, Hawai'i, were known for their beautifully designed ipus (gourds). However, the special techniques they used to make them were lost in time. Then, about twenty years ago, Dr. Bruce Ka'imiloa Chrisman discovered how they did it and taught the technique to artist Michael Harburg. Mr. Harburg kindly explained the process to me for this book.

What You Need to Dye an Ipu

1. Dye for your ipu. You can make a dye from instant coffee that gives a neat "old Hawai'i" look, or use Dharma fabric dye. Rit dye doesn't work well for this as it leaches out of the ipu. Do not add salt to your dye.

2. A sharp knife for scoring the ipu and cutting away the skin.

3. A scrubby for taking away dead skin.

4. A mature ipu.

5. A pen that will write on an ipu. Uni-ball® pens work well for this.

Steps to Dyeing an Ipu

1. Start with a mature ipu that has been just harvested. The stem should be brown and the gourd should be as hard as a dart board, but the skin should still be green. Take a pen

and draw the outline of your design on it. Make sure that the ink doesn't spread:

2. Take a knife with a pointed tip and score the gourd over the outline of your design:

3. Take a knife and carefully cut away the pieces of skin outside of the outline:

4. Wait about five days until the place where you cut off the skin has dried out. Then cut off the top of the gourd.

5. Now it is time to dye your ipu. The first step is to make your dye. The people of Ni'ihau made dyes from berries, leaves, or bark and water. They would put the dye mixture inside the dried-out gourd and let it sit until they felt that it had soaked up enough color. This takes about three to four weeks. By the time you are done, the skin on the outside of the gourd will be dead and even possibly a bit moldy. That's okay—it's still pulling the dye to the surface of the gourd.

6. Once you have finished dyeing your ipu, pour out the dye and rotten pulp and carefully clean out the inside.

7. Now, take a scrubby and rub away where you left the skin on (it is now dead skin). When you rub off the skin, you will see that the area underneath it will be the color of your dye. The skin has drawn the dye through the ipu, so that every place that you left the skin on shows color.

8. After you have dyed your ipu, you can polish it with kukui oil.

A Finished Ipu

Old Hawai'ian Games
By Pearl Dickson

The early Hawai'ians had many different games. In this article I will talk about five of them: Konane, 'Ulumaika, Moa pahe'e, Pala'ie, and Hu. Most Hawai'ian games were played to develop skill and strategy.

Konane (Hawai'ian Checkers)

Konane is not like European checkers. In European-style checkers, you have to capture as many of your opponent's pieces as possible, but when playing konane, your mission is to prevent your opponent from moving.

Materials Needed to Play Konane

To play konane you need some small black and white pebbles and a board that looks like this:

Konane Board

Konane boards can vary from very small to almost three feet long. The ancient Hawai'ians sometimes carved the holes for the game right into the lava. Some of these carved rocks can still be seen today.

How to Play Konane

First, you need to set up the board by placing alternating black and white pebbles into the holes:

The game is played with three players. Two of the players sit across from each other, and the third one is the referee. To start playing, the referee chooses one player to pick up one white pebble and one black pebble. The player puts the two pebbles behind his or her back, switches them around a little, and then holds them out in front with closed fists. The opponent has to choose a fist, and whichever color is in the fist that he chooses is the color that he will play with. The person with the black pebbles starts the game.

You move the rocks by jumping and "eating" each other, but you have to move into an empty space. For example if your opponent jumps over your pebble, he takes your piece, but HE HAS to land on an empty space when he jumps over your pebble. You can jump in any direction, except diagonally, but each move can only be in one direction. You can also jump over more than one piece at a time, but there has to be an empty space between each piece to land in. You can only move if there is a jump available to you, and you cannot jump over your own pieces.

The last player who is able to move is the victor, regardless of how many of the opponent's pieces he or she has collected.

'Ulumaika

'Ulumaika was a game used to develop skill and aim. It was usually played with a stone disk that was thicker in the middle than on the edges, though the Hawai'ians were also known to use half-grown breadfruit. The disk would be rolled on its edge like a wheel, and the object of the game was to roll the disk between the sticks.

To play ulumaika, you need a shaped lava stone and two stakes stuck in the ground about one foot or less apart:

To start, stand at least ten feet away from the stakes and try to roll your lava stone between the two stakes on the ground. Another variation of the game is to take a stone disk or ball, stand thirty to forty yards from the stakes, and try to toss the disk between the stakes without hitting them.

Moa Pahe'e

Moa Pahe'e is another game that helps with learning aim. It is similar to 'ulu maika because you have the two stakes as the goal.

To play moa pahe'e, you need two stakes lined up in the same way as in 'ulu maika, and a moa (wooden dart) that looks like this:

Hold the moa so that the fat end is facing the two stakes and the skinny end is facing you. Then stand at least ten to fifteen feet away from the stakes and try to slide the moa between the stakes without hitting them.

Pala'ie (Loop and Ball)

This is definitely a game to help you learn patience, but it is a fun game that can get very addicting! To play, first you need to make a loop out of coconut leaf ribs and attach it by a piece of twine to a ball made out of coconut fronds stuffed inside of a piece of cloth:

Once you have your loop and ball, you hang the ball by the string and try to toss it and catch it in the loop:

Hu (Spinning Top)

The kukui nut is best known as a source of oil for the ancient Hawai'ians. However, sometimes it had a less practical purpose.

Materials Needed to Make a Hu

A kukui nut
A rib from a coconut leaf that is about six inches long
A drill
Sandpaper

How to make a Hu

1. Pick some kukui nuts, husk them, and place them in a pot of water. Choose one that sinks to the bottom of the pot to be your top.

2. Using the sandpaper, sand the top of the nut flat. Then, take the drill and drill a small hole in the top of the nut to put the coconut leaf rib in. Be careful not to split the kukui nut in half. The hole should go at least half way through the nut.

3. Take your coconut leaf rib and stick it through the hole in your kukui nut. Make sure you stick the coconut rib all the way down to the bottom of the hole.

4. You need a flat surface to spin it on. If it falls down, chop off some of the coconut rib a little at a time, until it spins perfectly for you. Below is a photo of a hu, but the frond on yours could end up shorter or longer, depending on what works best for you. Now spin it and have fun!

Hawai'ian Lei Making
By Emily Risley

Lei making is an ancient Hawai'ian craft that plays a major part in Hawai'ian ceremonies and everyday life. Depending on the occasion, a lei can be used to express gratitude, congratulations, or condolences. They are given at weddings, funerals, birthdays, and graduations, and are used as ways to say thank you, hello, and goodbye. In short, leis represent a physical form of aloha, a word which can mean love, hello, goodbye, and unity.

Lei Styles

There are five types of leis:

1) Lei kui, consisting of a thread or vine on which flowers have been strung.

A Lei Kui Made of Dried Orchids

2) Lei hua, which is similar to the lei kui, only with seeds instead of flowers.

A Lei Hua Made of Kukui Nuts

3) Lei haku, which is a simple lei of braided leaves, usually adorned with flowers.

A Lei Haku Made of Braided Ti Leaves

4) Lei kipu'u, a long lei of vines which drape across one's shoulders and is open at the ends.

A Lei Kipu'u

5) Lei wili, a lei which has a main band with flowers and foliage tied onto the band by a piece of string.

A Lei Wili

Materials

Materials for leis vary widely, and pretty much any type of non-poisonous plant can be used. However a lei maker must take into account the durability and appropriateness of the plant. As certain plants have certain meanings, Hawai'ian lei makers are careful about the materials that they use in their leis. Some plants that are often used are:

Ferns- Ferns are most generally used in lei wili, and are great as a kind of background for a lei.

Plumeria- The fragrant and beautiful blossoms can be used in any lei, but are most common in lei kui.

Kukui- Both the leaves and nuts of the kukui tree are a great addition to a lei.

In general, fragrant flowers such as the pikake and tuber rose are especially fun and colorful to work with.

Some materials that are especially hard to work with are: small flowers; flowers with delicate petals; plants which have a short life span once picked; and flowers with intricate formations, such as orchids and birds of paradise.

Designing the Lei

When designing a lei, the lei maker must take into account what the lei is for. For example, a hula dancer would want a lei that matches his or her costume and helps to illustrate the story. A lei given to someone who has strength or willpower may include 'a'ali'i. Likewise, hala fruit can symbolize either a person taking on a new task or death, while kukui leaves represent knowledge. Brown foliage is just as good as green foliage, and one can be used to accent the other.

Making the Lei

The early Hawai'ians made leis with cord made of olonā, 'ie'ie, or other plant fibers and a needle made from a coconut palm frond rib. However, today most people opt for a more modern method and use a metal needle with thread or raffia.

To make a lei kui, you only need some flowers, thread, and needle. Loop the thread through the needle and tie a knot on the other end. Then string on flowers to the desired length and tie the ends together. A lei hua is made the same way, only using seeds instead of flowers.

To make a lei haku, simply braid together leaves (ti leaves are good for this) braiding the stems of flowers in at the desired points.

To make a lei kipu'u, entwine and tie vines until the desired length is reached. Leave the ends open.

Making a lei wili is more complicated. First gather your materials. For the following example we used:

Ti Leaves

Ferns

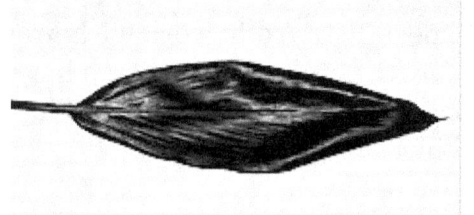
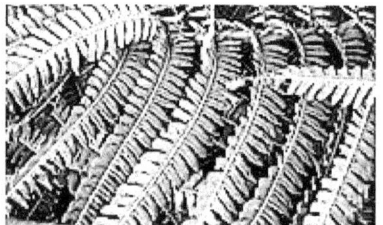

Kukui Leaves

'A'ali'i blossom clusters

You will also need raffia and string to tie it all together.

Steps to Make a Lei Wili

1) To figure out how long your lei needs to be, measure the head, wrist, or ankle that the lei is for, then add two or three inches to your measurement.

2) Cut or rip several ti leaves in half along the midrib:

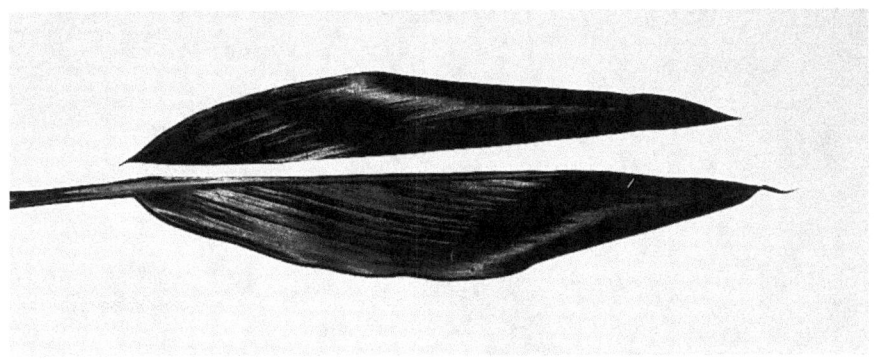

3) Place the two halves of each ti leaf atop each other:

4) Fold the edges of the long side of the ti leaves under, creating a rectangular shape:

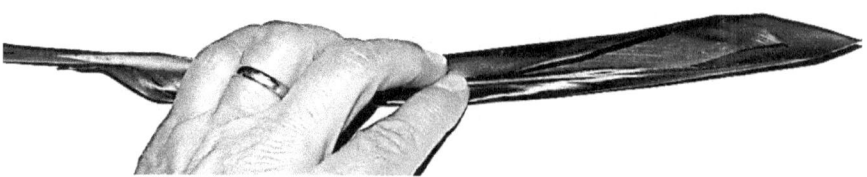

5) Take one long piece of raffia (or thread) and tie it to one end of the ti leaf. Leave a tail at the end. This tail will be used later to tie the lei on when it comes time to wear it.

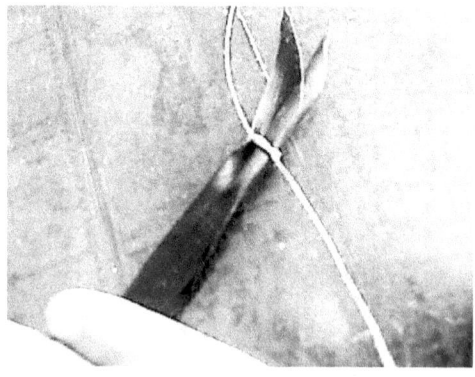

6) Place the first piece or bunch of foliage on top of the smooth side of the ti leaf. (The folded side of the ti leaf should be facing down.) Wrap the raffia around its stem until it feels secure:

7) Add more foliage on and continue wrapping, placing each piece on top of the previous wrap so that the raffia is hidden:

Every so often, bend the lei backwards with the greenery facing towards you. If you can see the ti leaf underneath, there needs to be more foliage. Remember to wrap everything on tight, so that it does not fall off.

To make the lei longer, add on more ti leaves by overlapping them with the current leaves, and then continue wrapping.

8) To finish it off, loop the raffia around the ti leaf and stick the end of the string through the last loop:

9) Finally, pull it tight, leaving a loop:

Use this loop and the tail of string at the other end of the lei to tie it on. If the lei is not going to be in use for a while, it's a good idea to store it in the refrigerator.

The art of lei making is diverse and widespread. Many island cultures make leis, and while some are similar, there are many different styles. Hawai'ian leis are especially pretty, with all of their unique flowers and greenery.

Fishing in Old Hawai'i
By Dylan Kilbride

Fish were an important source of protein in Hawai'i, and the Hawai'ians had many unique and creative ways of catching them. Their methods varied depending on the number or type of fish being caught.

One of these methods was the hukilau. This was a fishing method where a whole community or group of people would go out into a bay carrying a rope with ti leaves hanging from it. The rope could be as much as a quarter of a mile long. They would use the rope to form a half-circle around the opening of the bay. Once everyone was in place, the people on the edges would slowly start pulling the net toward the shallows, while the people in the middle would shake the leaves and make noises to scare the fish. As the net was pulled closer to the shore, the fish would be trapped between the people and the land and could be scooped up with nets or even by hand. The name hukilau came from the Hawai'ian words *huki*, which means pull, and *lau*, which means leaves.

This fishing method was a way to catch a lot of fish at one time and was only used for special occasions as it required a large number of people.

A section of a Hukilau Net

The early Hawai'ians also used fish hooks (makau) and line, much like we do today. One of the methods they used was to take a long line that had fish hooks strung on it and a stone sinker tied to one end. The sinkers used for this were heavy–the average weight was about three and a half pounds. They would lower the line down into the water and let the fish bite. Once enough fish were biting, the fisherman would pull the line up. Since the Hawai'ians did not use fishing poles, they would pull the line up by hand and use nets to scoop up the fish. This method was mainly used for deep sea fishing.

Hooks were made out of bone, wood, turtle shell and mother-of pearl. They mostly used human bone or dog bone, but they also used whale bone for larger hooks. Human thigh bones were particularly popular. The Hawai'ians believed that hooks made from the bones of individuals with no hair on their bodies were more attractive to the fish.

There were many different designs for the hooks, depending on what fish was being caught. Some hooks also had shark teeth attached to the tips. Following is a description of one of the ways the Hawai'ians attached a hook to the line. Fishing line was often made from olonā plant fibers.

How to Attach a Hook to a Leader

Hooks are first attached to a string called a leader, and the leader is later attached to the fishing line. To attach a hook to a leader, you will need a hook, a long thick line for your leader, another line that is about eighteen inches long, a knife, and a thin

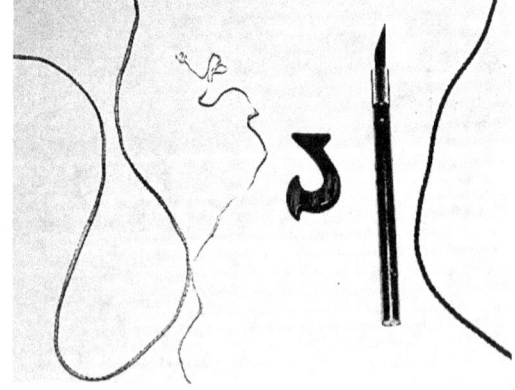

piece of thread that is about eight inches long (dental floss works especially well for this).

First, take your leader line and loop it over the shank of the hook:

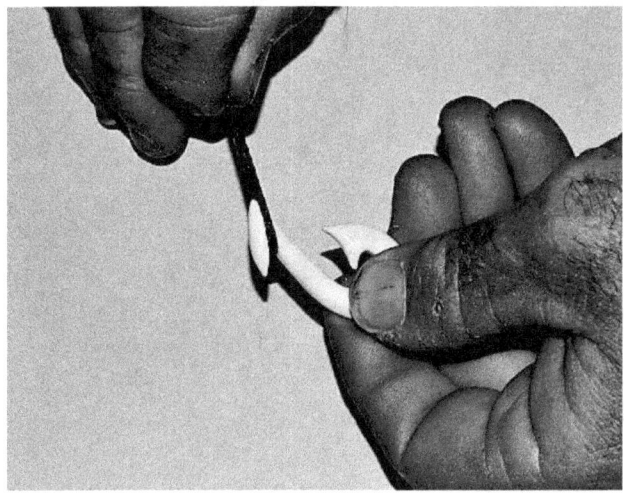

Then have someone hold the other end, putting tension on the line:

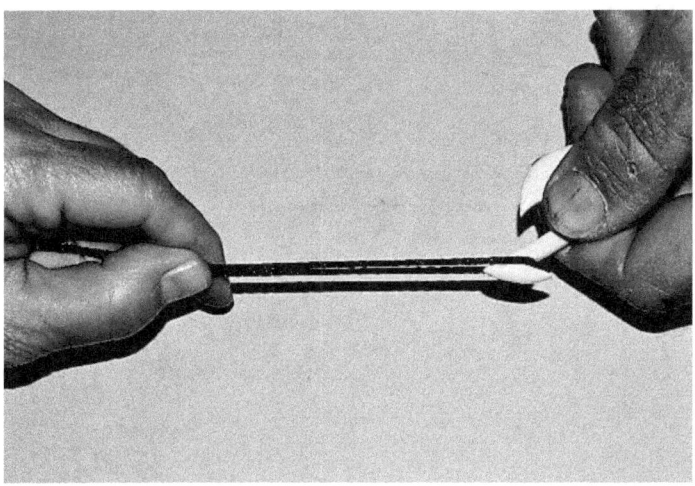

For a small fish hook, take another piece of line that is at least eighteen inches long and put one end against the fish hook and alongside the leader line:

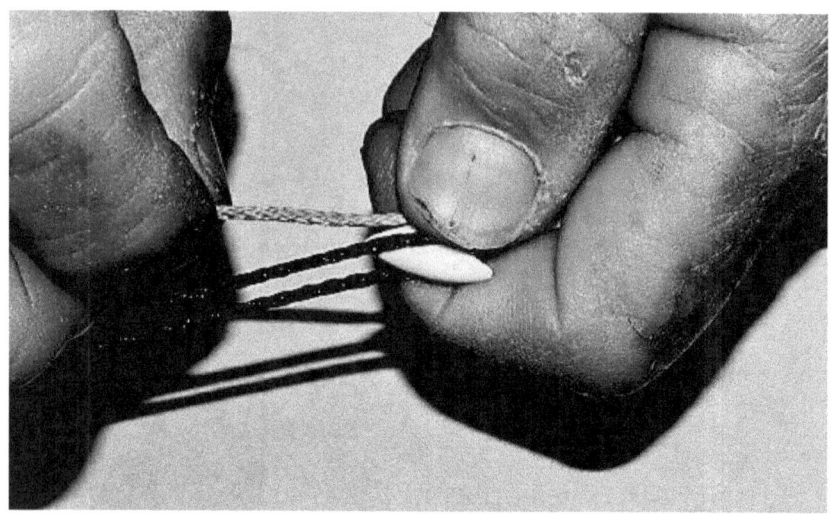

Take the new line and form a loop over both sides of the leader line and wrap it around:

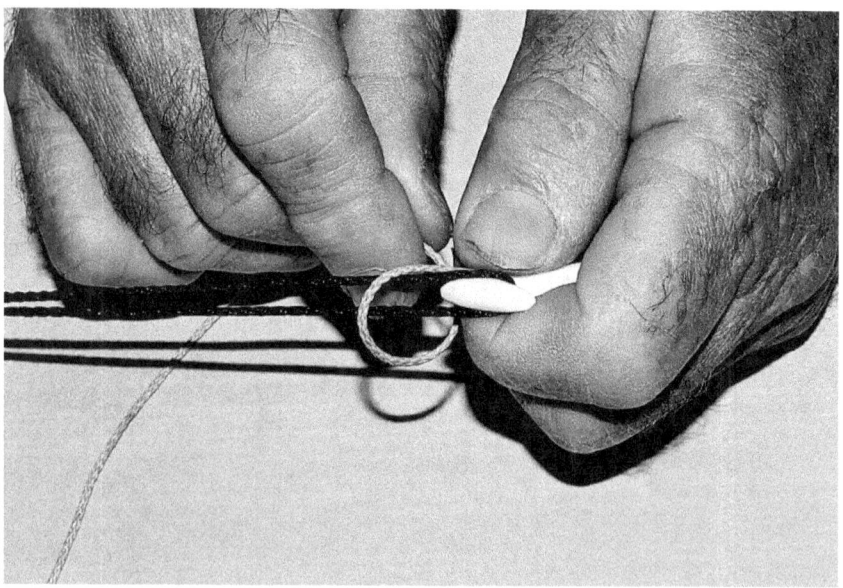

Continue wrapping around the leader line, pulling tight and staying close to each wrap:

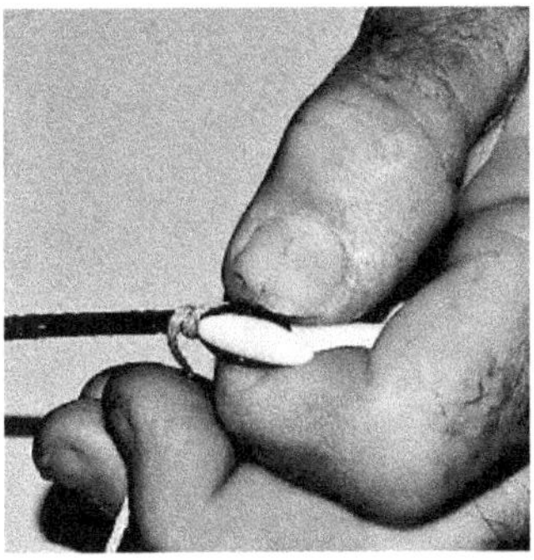

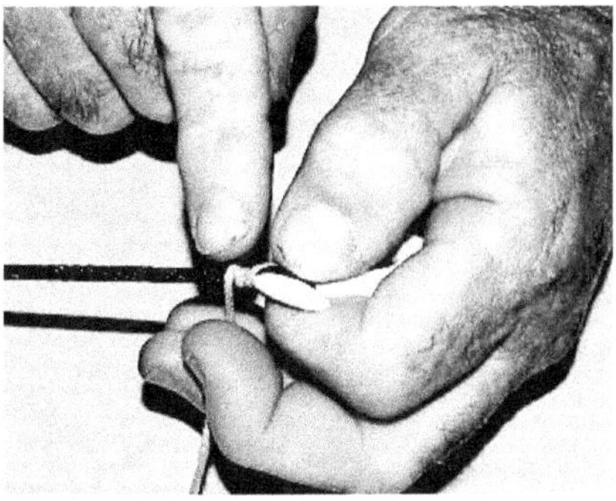

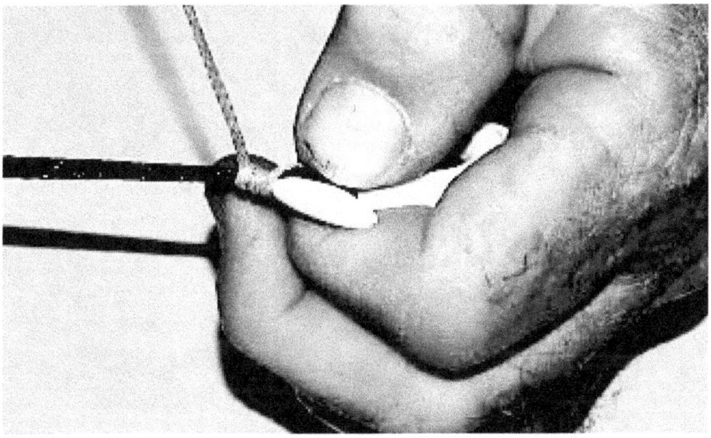

After five wraps away from the hook, begin wrapping back toward the hook, holding everything tight and keeping close to each previous wrap:

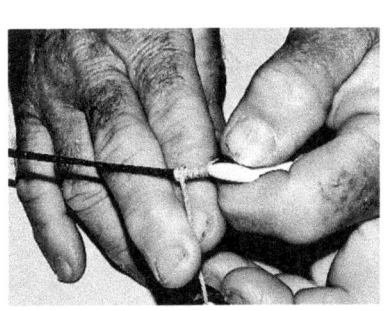
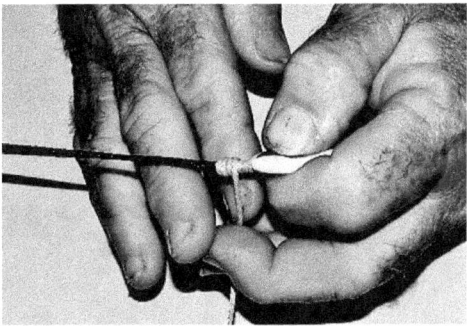

When you get back to the fishhook, continue wrapping over the end of the hook, keeping your wraps tight, until about three turns *onto* the fishhook:

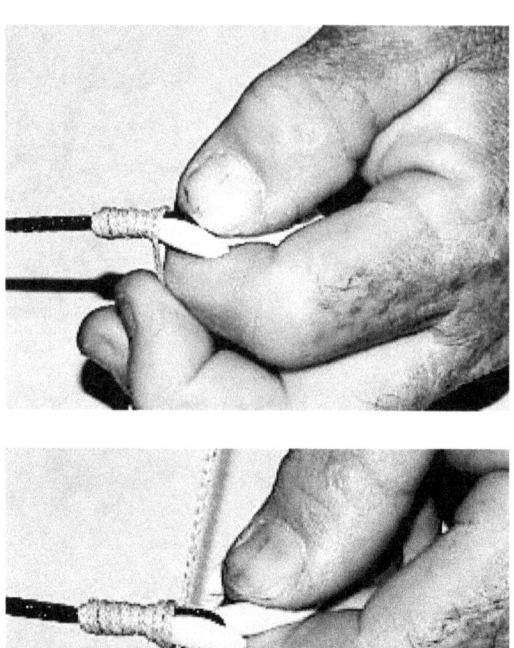

Now begin a figure-eight pattern, first going under the other end of the top of the hook:

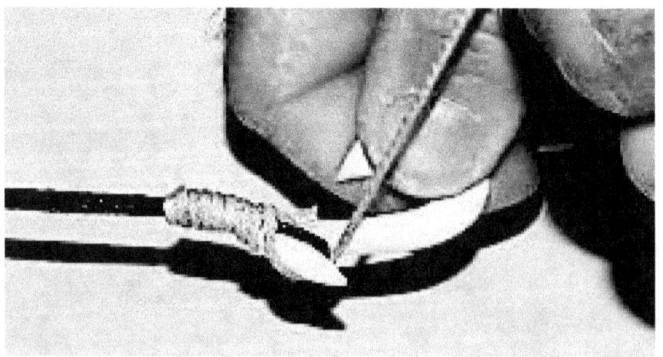

And up and over toward the opposite side:

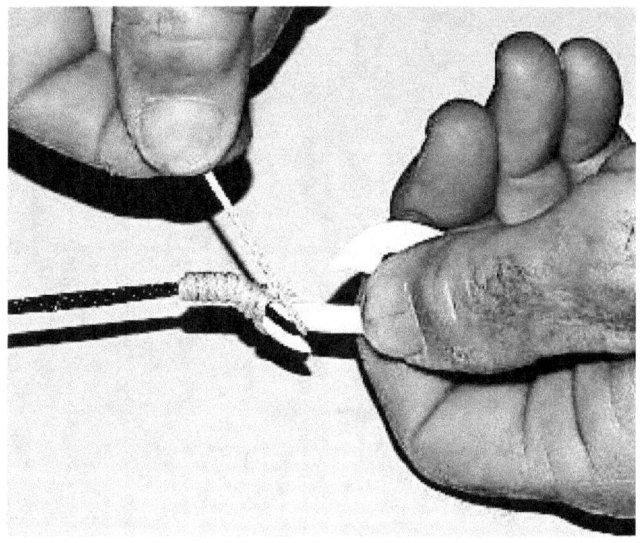

Then under:

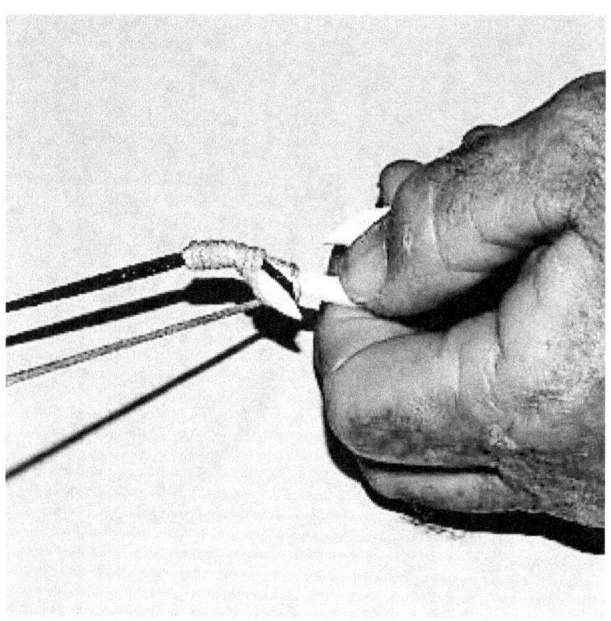

And over the top:

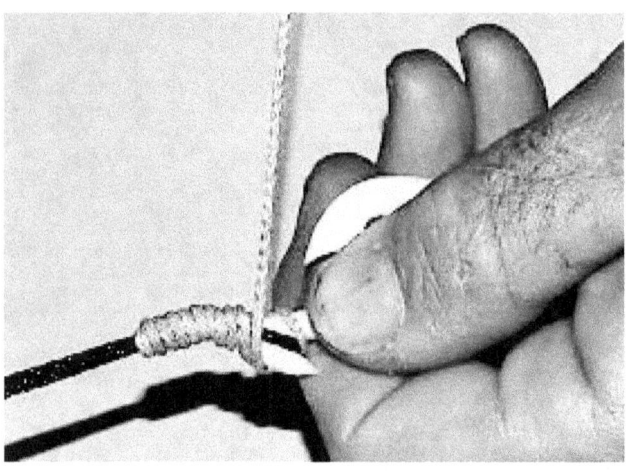

Repeat this pattern, keeping everything tight and snug:

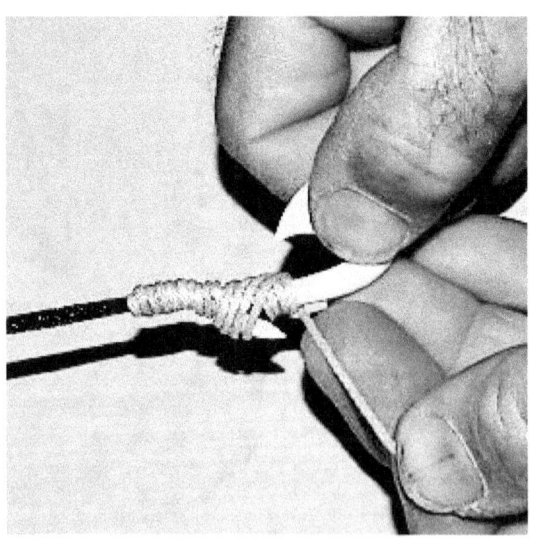

Stop when you have covered most, but not all, of the tip on the top of the hook:

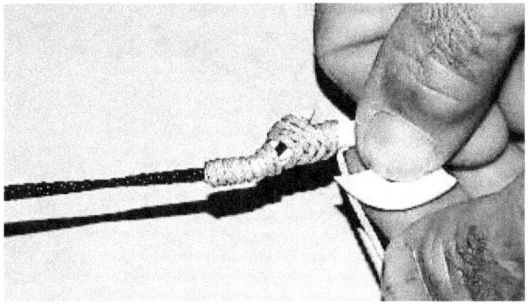

To lock the line in, take a thin piece of line (dental floss works well for this) and form a loop. Lay the loop down on the shank of the hook:

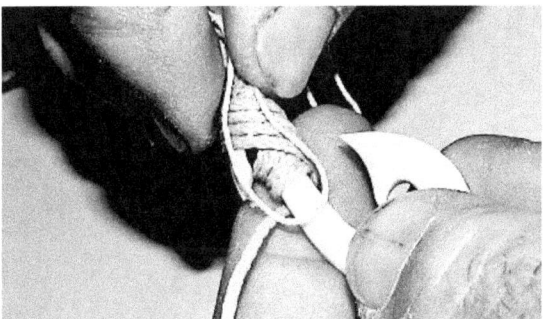

Start to wrap the rest of your line down the shank and on top of the loop for about three turns:

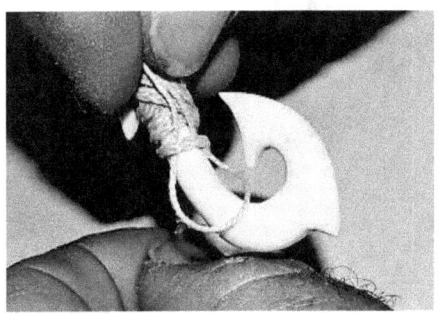 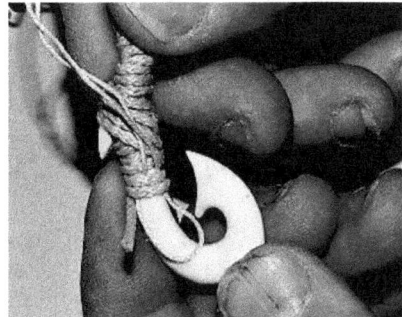

Pass the free end of your line through the loop:

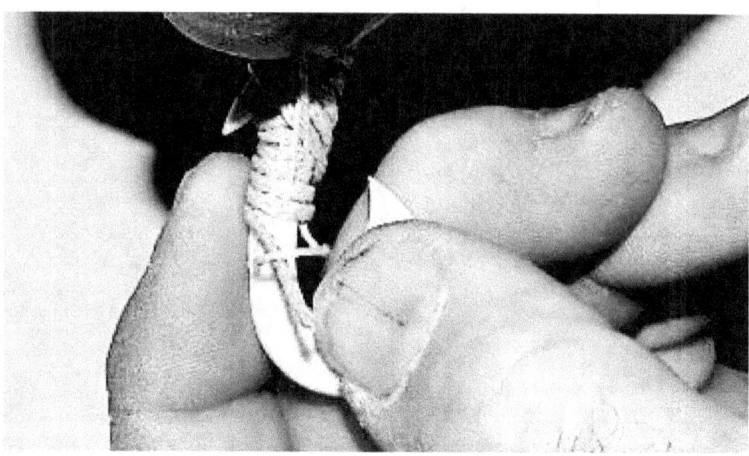

Now pull on the free ends of the loop, which will pull the end of your line under the wraps. To secure it, you may need to wiggle it a little to get it through:

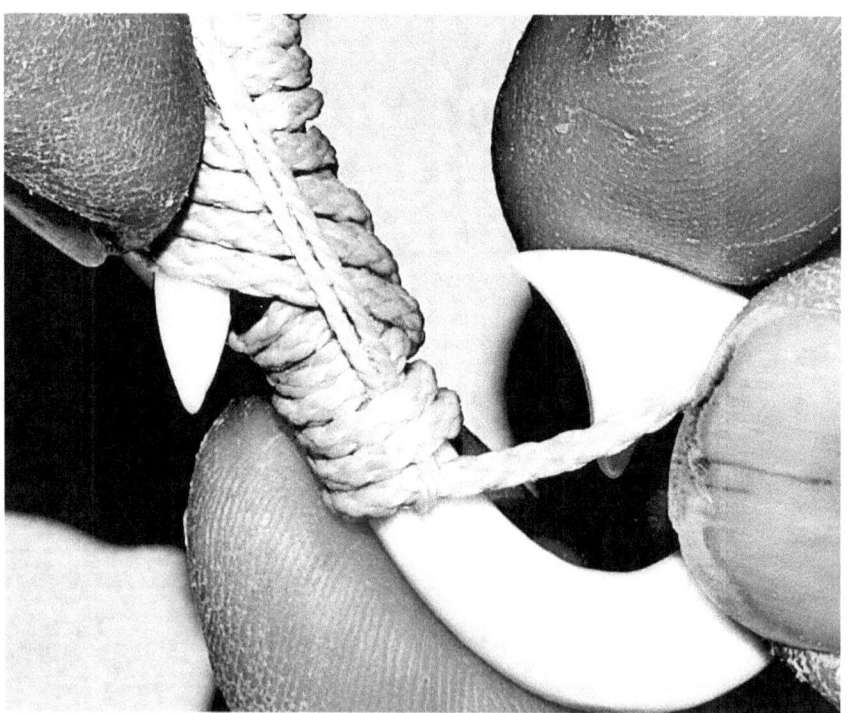

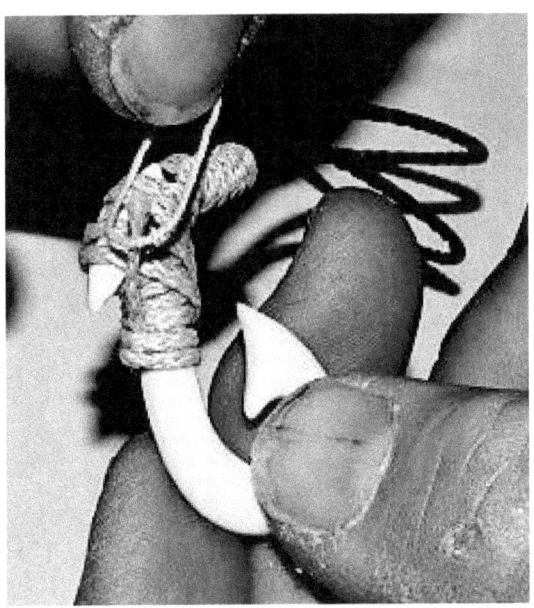
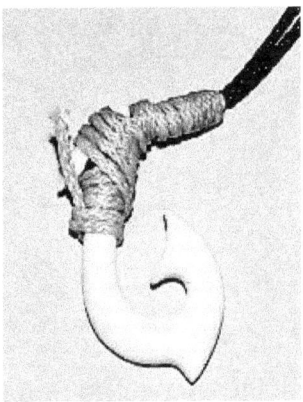

Take a knife and carefully slice the end close to the wraps. Be very careful not to slice the wraps themselves:

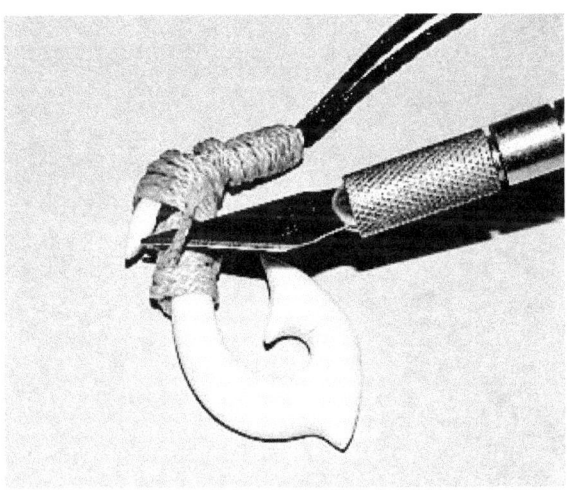

If you are using nylon line, you can also take a match and either heat up the blade of the knife, or use the match itself to melt the end of the line.

You now have a fish hook attached to a leader. The other end of the leader is what you attach to the fishing line:

The hook in the picture above is a pretty standard one. However, a special type of hook and lure was used to catch octopus. It was made of a large fish hook that was attached to one end of a stick. The other end of the stick was placed in a groove that had been cut into a stone and a cowrie shell was placed on top. The end of the stick near the hook had plant fibers sticking out past the hook to form a brush.*

*Octopus lure and parts courtesy of Hawai'i Parks Association

The photo below shows some of the pieces that make up an octopus lure.

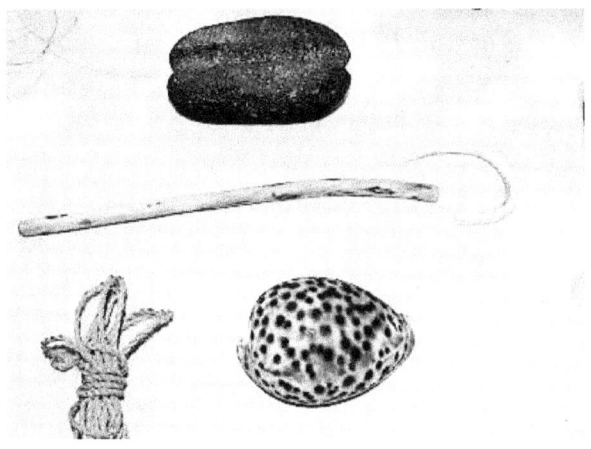

To use the lure, first the fisherman would chew kukui nuts and spit them in the water. The oil from the nuts would smooth the surface of the water so that the fisherman could see down to the ocean bottom. Once he ascertained where an octopus was, the fisherman would take the lure and lower it down to the bottom, waiting for the octopus to come near it.

When an octopus got close to the lure, the fisherman would move the lure very slowly–so that it was moving like a snail. Once the octopus started to follow the lure, the fisherman would slowly pull the lure a little bit off the ocean floor. To keep the octopus interested, the fisherman would tickle the octopus with the brush on the end of the lure. The octopus would then grab onto the cowrie shell, and the fisherman would slowly pull the line up towards the surface. At some point the octopus would usually realize the shell was empty, and start to back down off the cowrie. It would feel the hook and wrap itself over it to see what it was. That was when the fisherman would jerk up on the line and catch the octopus.

The octopus lure is a good example of how the Hawai'ian fishermen's understanding of the behavior of their prey helped them to catch fish.

Another way hooks were used was with various types of bait. The bait was either placed on the fishhook or sprinkled in the water around the boat. There were also special sticks called la'au melomelo that served as bait. They were one to three feet long with one rounded end. The other end had a small knob at the top to tie a line to. A La'au melomelo was first carved out of hard wood that was so heavy that it sank in water, and then it was charred over a fire. Finally, it was rubbed with coconut or kukui nut oil. The oily stick was let down into the water until the fish came to it. Then it was slowly drawn up toward the boat, where the stick was guided into a bag-shaped net. Once the net was full of fish, it was drawn shut and lifted onto the boat.

The early Hawai'ians had a variety of nets that they used. One interesting type was the dip net. It was a net suspended from two bent and crossed sticks. To use it, first a fish was caught and tied with a string through its mouth and gills so it was still alive and could swim. The fisherman would have it swim next to other fish of the same species. Then the fisherman would carefully pull the fish on the line toward the net, and the other fish would follow it right into the net. When a large amount of fish had collected in the net, the fishermen would pull up on it, and the weight of the fish in the net would cause the sticks to bend, closing the net around the fish.

Throw nets were introduced to Hawai'i by the Japanese. A throw net is a circular net with weights on the outer part of the circle. It is thrown into the water so that it opens up and floats to the bottom, trapping a school of fish underneath it. Then the fisherman pulls on a rope, drawing the net around the fish and pulling the net up.

While throw nets are more recent nets, the very earliest Hawai'ian nets were probably fish traps. Fish traps were used to catch fish while the fisherman was away doing other tasks. They were designed so the entrance of the trap allowed fish in, but not back out again. They were often placed in freshwater streams, where the fish would be able to swim in, but the current and the shape of the trap would prevent them from swimming back out.

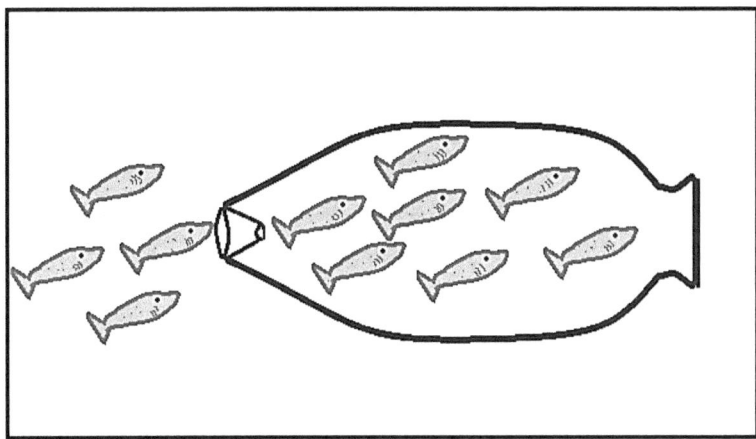

Another fishing method was to use spears. They were made out of hard wood with a jagged tip. Spears were often used at night with torches in rocky shallow areas. They were also used to catch porcupine fish and octopus.

These are just a few of the many Hawai'ian fishing methods. Fishing in Hawai'i was a very important art that required an extensive knowledge of fish behavior.

How to Weave an Eke i'a
(Fish Basket)
By Hope Mashburn

Ancient Hawai'ians who lived inland would use eke i'a or fish baskets made out of lau niu (coconut leaves) to carry their catch back to their villages. Since eke i'a were woven so that they were watertight, the Hawai'ians could put water into the baskets with the fish so that the fish would stay alive and not spoil on the long trek home.

Before you make an eke i'a, you first have to know some basics about coconut leaves:

Parts of Lau Niu (Coconut Leaves)

Great midrib

Envelope

Tapered end

Wide end

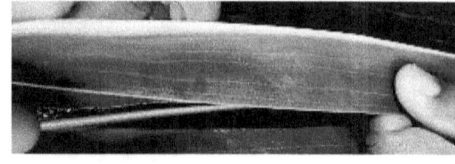

To make an eke i'a, carefully follow the steps below:

1. Take a coconut palm frond and split it down the center of the midrib:

2. Lay one section on top of the other. Then cut the sections so that you end up with two pieces of the palm frond that have six leaflets each:

3. Shave off part of the thick midrib:

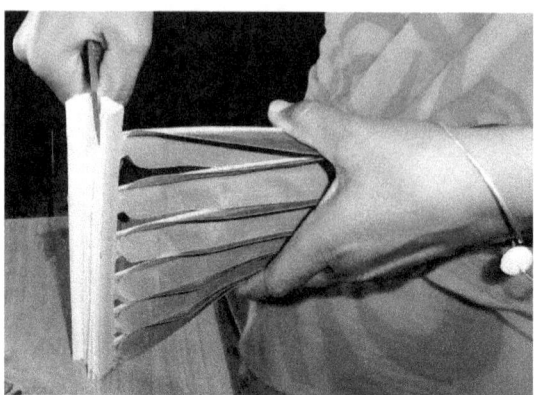

4. Cut the leaves into two sets of three:

5. Put into matching pairs:

6. Start with your first matching pair. Match the great midribs together so that the leaves form the letter "V":

7. Hold the mid ribs as in the picture above and turn the ends of the leaves without mid ribs inward so that they form the letter X, **with the left frond over the right**. To start the weaving process, take the first leaflet on the left, closest to you, and go over, under, and over the leaflet on the right. Notice that the leaf envelopes are closed at this point:

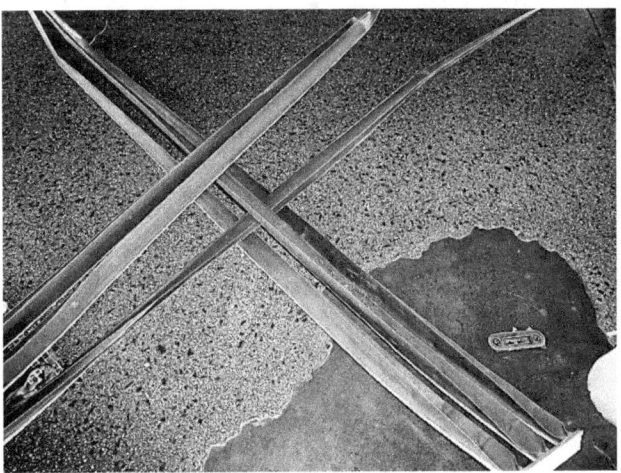

8. The second leaflet on the left goes under, over, and under the three leaflets on the right – the opposite of the first leaflets that you wove. The third leaflet is the same as the first:

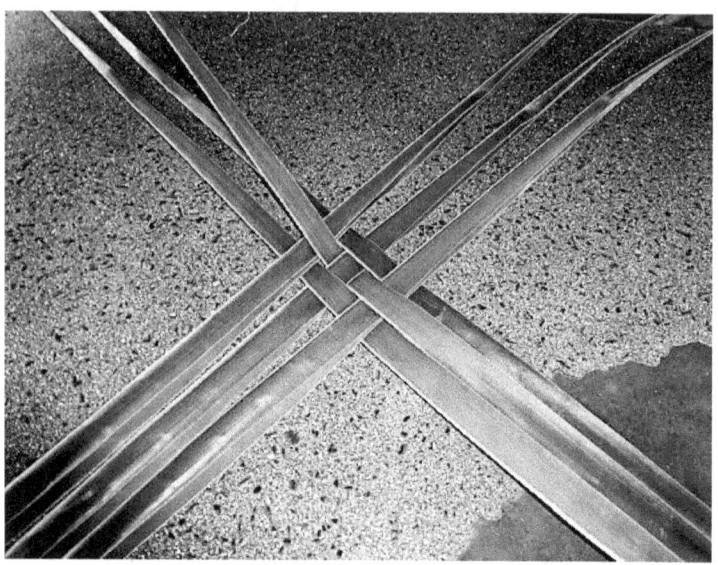

9. Now open all six envelopes:

10. Tighten up the envelopes together and slide everything down closer to the great midribs. Give yourself about three inches of space between the great midrib and the first leaf on each side:

11. Set this project to the side and grab your next pair. Repeat the weaving process.

12. You should now have two sets of woven leaves:

13. Take one set of leaves and place them in front of you so that one mid rib is to the left and one is on the bottom:

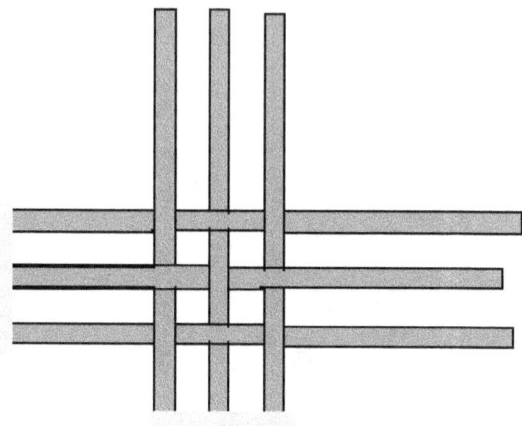

14. Take the other set of leaves and place them directly on top of the first leaves, but the top set of leaves should have one mid rib on the right and one at the top:

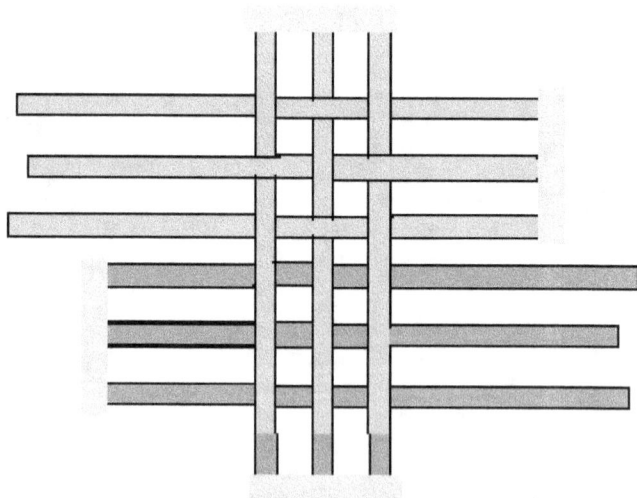

15. Now, move the top set of leaves over a bit to the right, so that the vertical leaves are lined up alongside each other. (And the horizontal leaves should also be lined up alongside each other.)

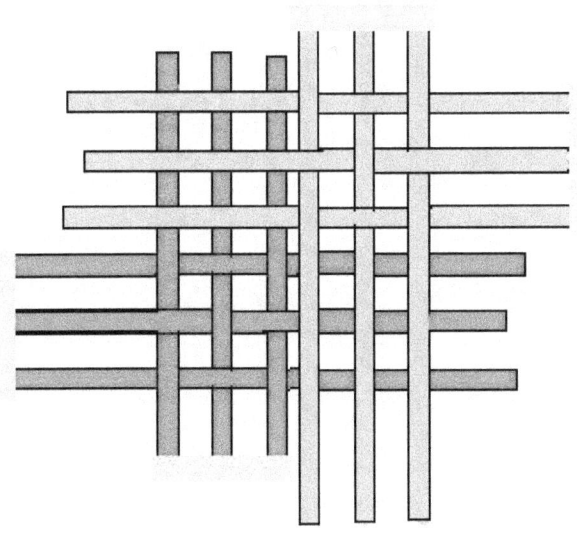

16. Now weave the fronds together here:

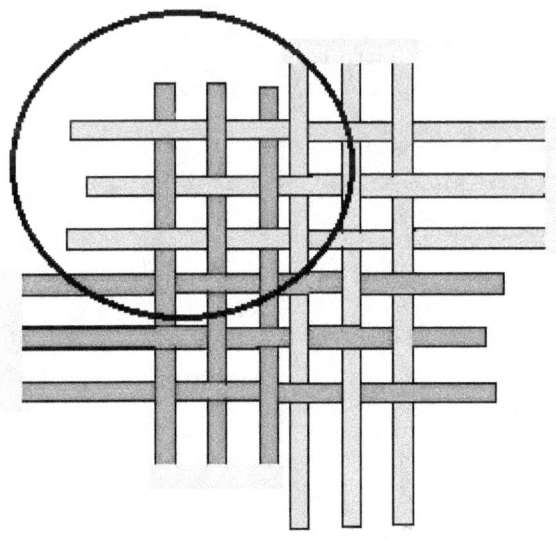

17. Next, weave the fronds together here:

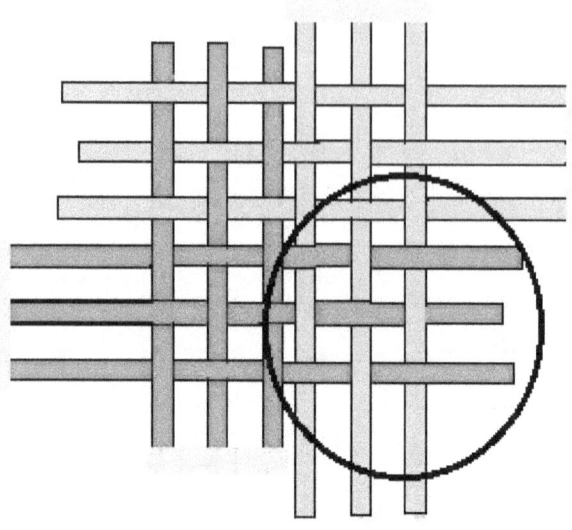

18. You should now have something that looks like this:

19. It is time to start weaving the sides. Put the project into your lap, placing a pico against your stomach. A pico is where two sets of leaves come together in a valley. In the picture below, the pico is between leaves three and four. Choose a pico that does not have a mid-rib section as one of its sides. Once you have the pico against your stomach, you should see the same pattern of leaves in the following photo out in front of you:

20. Leaflets three, five, and six will be woven to the left. Leaflet three goes over leaflet two, under leaflet one, and through the mid rib section using the same pattern:

21. Take leaflet five and also weave it to the left, doing the opposite weave pattern of leaflet three:

22. Take leaflet six and do the same pattern that you did with leaflet three, also weaving to the left:

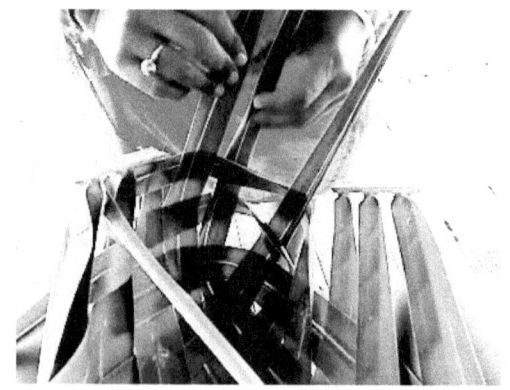

23. Take leaflets four, two, and one, (in that order) and weave them to the *right*:

24. Pinch the two top great mid ribs together and tighten the weaving that you just did:

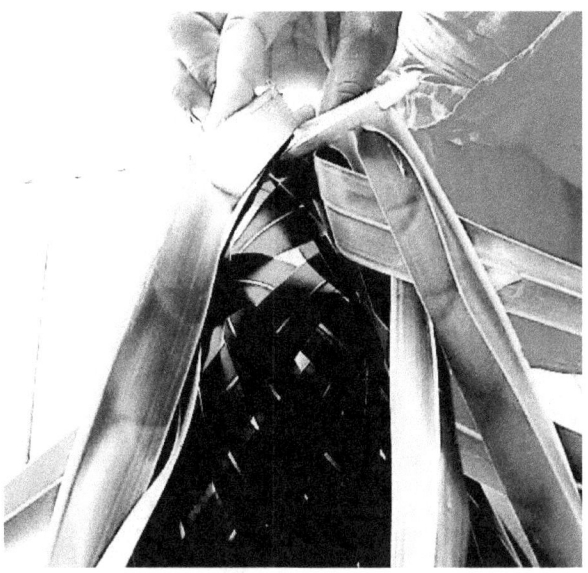

25. Tie an easy knot with the excess from the six fronds you were just weaving to keep them out of your way. Repeat the same weaving process on other end of basket:

26. Take the three tips on each corner and braid them separately. Finish the end of each braid with a knot:

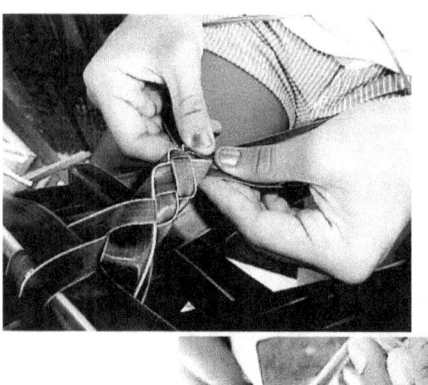

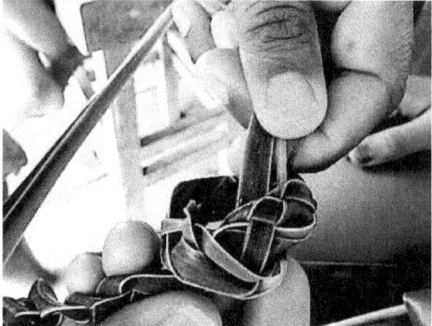

27. Next, tie your braids together to create handles....

And your eke i'a is complete!

A Bamboo Percussion Instrument
By Charlee Brown

The 'ohe ka 'eke 'eke, sometimes called a ka 'eke 'eke, is a drum that consists of two bamboo pipes that you pound on the ground to make a rhythm. The early Hawai'ians used this bamboo instrument for hula dances, entertainments, and ceremonies.

The first step in making an 'ohe ka 'eke 'eke is to harvest the bamboo. The best time to harvest bamboo is after the rainy season and before the dry season. If you don't harvest it at the proper time, it will deteriorate much faster than bamboo that is harvested at the correct time of the year.

You have to be very careful when cutting down bamboo. It is easy to damage through improper harvesting. Two basic rules when cutting bamboo are: don't drag the bamboo after cutting it (to prevent stains), and don't let the bamboo drop on hard ground (to prevent cracking).

Items Needed to Make an 'Ohe Ka 'Eke 'Eke

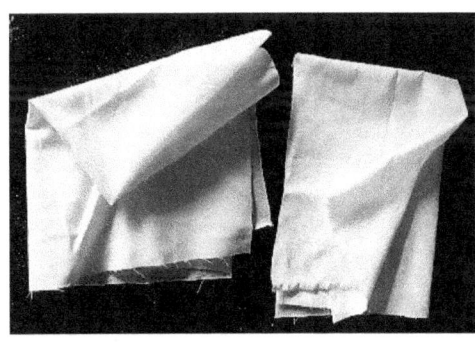

Two Cloths

**Two Bamboo Pipes
(each closed at one end)**

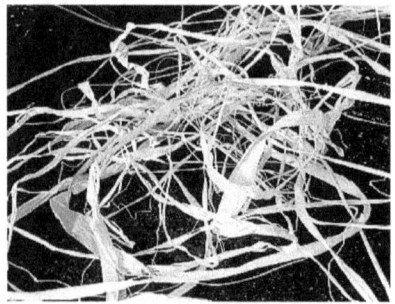 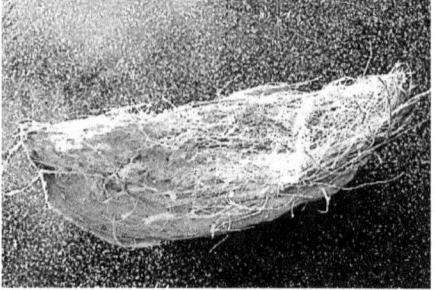

String or Twine   **Coconut Husk**

Steps to Make an 'Ohe Ka 'Eke 'Eke

Remove some fibers from the coconut husk and place them on top of the closed end of one of your bamboo pieces–to form sort of a pillow. Do this to each of the bamboo pieces. The fibers help to protect the bamboo. Don't pack it too tight or else the sound will muffle.

Next, put the cloth over the coconut fibers. You need to do this on each of the bamboo tubes:

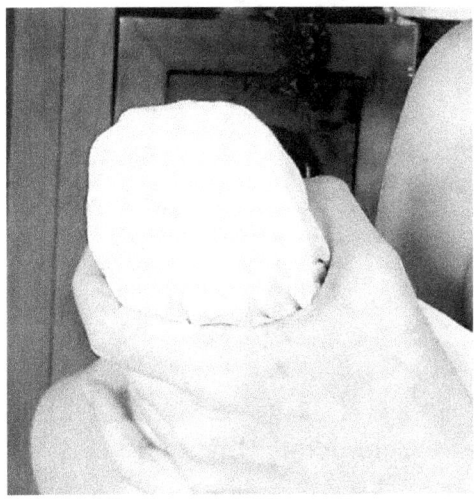

Take your string or twine and tie it around the bamboo a couple of times, then double knot it:

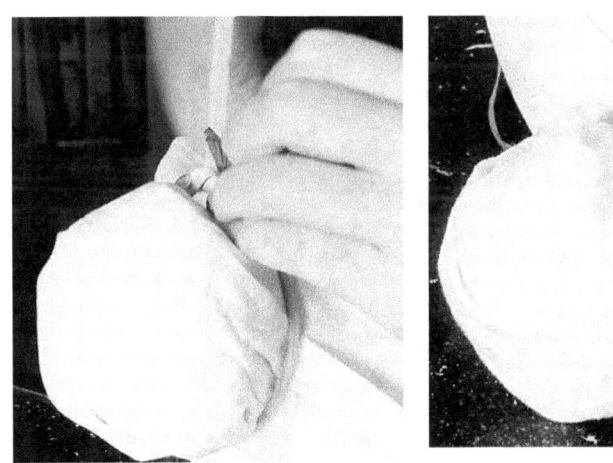

Follow these steps on both of the pieces of bamboo.

Completed 'Ohe Ka 'Eke 'Eke

People usually sit while playing the drums. They lightly strike the ground in a rhythm or hit the two bamboo tubes together. The tones produced will depend on the size of the tubes.

Early Hawai'ian Weapons
By Dylan Kilbride

I recently had the opportunity to interview Hawai'ian weapons maker Stan Hein at his shop in Kona, Hawai'i. He has been studying and making ancient Hawai'ian weapons for a number of years.

When I asked Stan what were the most common early Hawai'ian weapons, he replied that the most common weapons were the spear and the club. Most of the fighters were ordinary soldiers, and spears and clubs were the easiest weapons to find and make. Clubs were usually very simple, just a thick hard root, or a tree branch with a rock tied to the top. There were also more complex clubs made with sharks' teeth, which were usually used by royalty.

**Photo of a Hawai'ian Club
Courtesy of the
King Kamehameha Hotel**

A More Complex Club Made with Shark's Teeth

There were two different methods of attaching shark teeth to the clubs. One was the peg method, where the teeth had holes drilled in them and were pegged in. In the other method, the teeth were lashed to the club. Stan told me that the peg method was more efficient, because if a tooth fell out, you could just peg a new one right in. With the lashing method, if a tooth was broken, it had to be completely unstrung and then restrung again.

A Shark's Tooth Club Made Using the Peg Method

A Shark's Tooth Club Made Using the Lashing Method

Spears, the other common weapon used by Hawai'ian warriors, were up to fourteen feet long. The type of wooden spear shown below was carved so that when the tip broke off, the next piece would still be sharp. This would increase the damage of the wound as the tip would remain imbedded in the wound, and the next tip would be ready for use.

Sketch of an Early Hawai'ian Spear

If this tip breaks off,

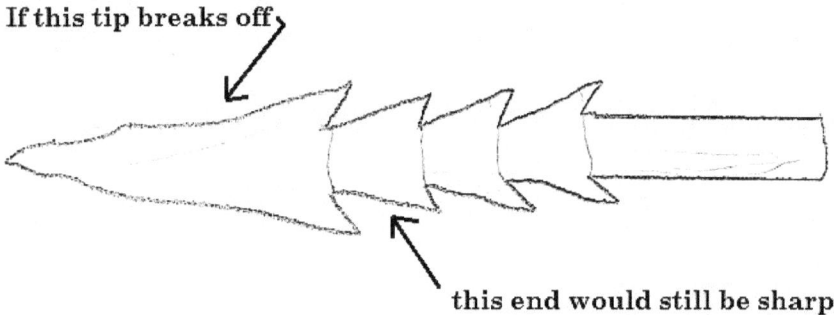

this end would still be sharp.

Another type of weapon used by the early Hawai'ians was the knuckle duster, which was made to fit on a warrior's hand. Knuckle dusters were imbedded with shark's teeth.

Knuckle Duster

According to Stan, the early Hawai'ians probably used different types of sharks' teeth in their weapons. Tiger Shark teeth were used, but they may have used Bull Shark teeth and even Great White Shark teeth occasionally. Basically, if they caught a shark, they would have used its teeth. One shark could supply a weapon maker with many teeth, because their jaws have many replacement teeth in case one falls out.

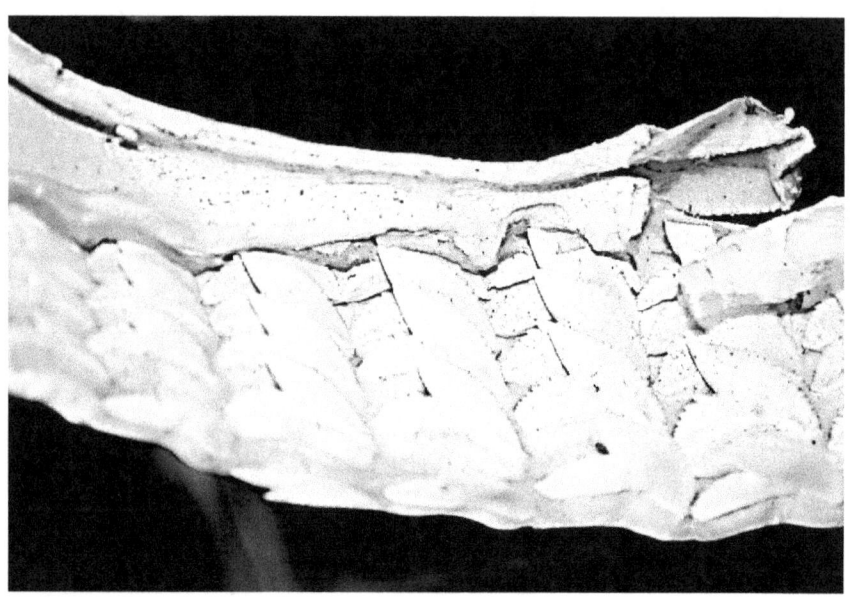

Part of a Shark's Jaw with the Rows of Teeth Ready to Emerge

Next, I asked Stan if the early Hawai'ians used weapons for hunting. He replied, "Not really," because the early Hawai'ians didn't do a lot of hunting. Their pigs were domesticated, so they didn't need to hunt them. The chiefs used bow and arrows for hunting rats, but that was about it. They didn't usually use the bows in battle either.

The early Hawai'ians also made swords and daggers. One type of sword was made from swordfish bills. They were very strong and were used for stabbing.

A Sword Made from a Swordfish Bill

I asked Stan if they sharpened the Swordfish bill swords, and he said they may have sharpened them. He also mentioned that they were very hard to break due to the honeycomb structure of the bill, so they were very strong.

The Internal Structure of a Swordfish Bill

When I asked Stan what types of wood the early Hawai'ians used to make their weapons, he told me that koa was the most commonly used wood, but that they used different types of wood for different weapons. They used kauila for daggers and olopua for spears. Other woods used were kou, uhi-uhi, and ulei.

The early Hawai'ians made other weapons besides the daggers, swords, and clubs that Stan specializes in. For example, they also made slings, tripping stones, and canoe crashers.

Canoe crashers were large heavy stones with cords attached to them that were used in naval battles. They were thrown at the enemy canoes and then hauled back with the cord to be used again.

Tripping stones were two stones connected by a rope. They were thrown at an enemy's legs to trip him, making him an easy target.

The slings were woven out of fibers, including the part where the rock was held.

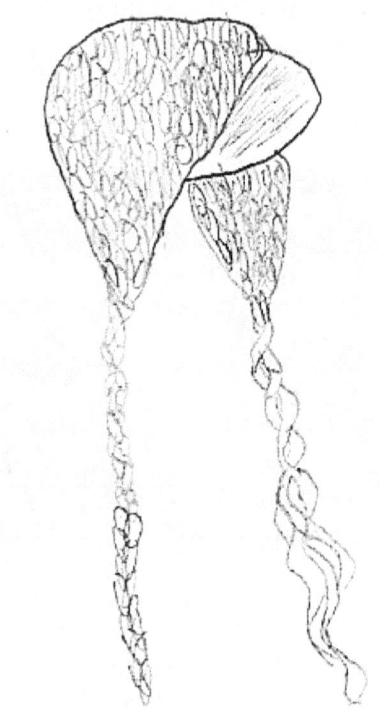

Sketch of a Sling with a Rock in It

Hawai'i is one of the few Pacific islands where there are early records of dagger use. Many early Hawai'ian daggers had a loop that would slip over the user's wrist.

How to Make a Marlin Bill Dagger

A number of sources mention that the early Hawai'ians made marlin-bill daggers. I made the one described below based on some of their descriptions. However, I did not have authentic directions on how to make it.

A Marlin Bill

To make the dagger, take a marlin bill and place a piece of cord on it, as shown in the photo below. In the finished dagger, the loop will go over the user's wrist.

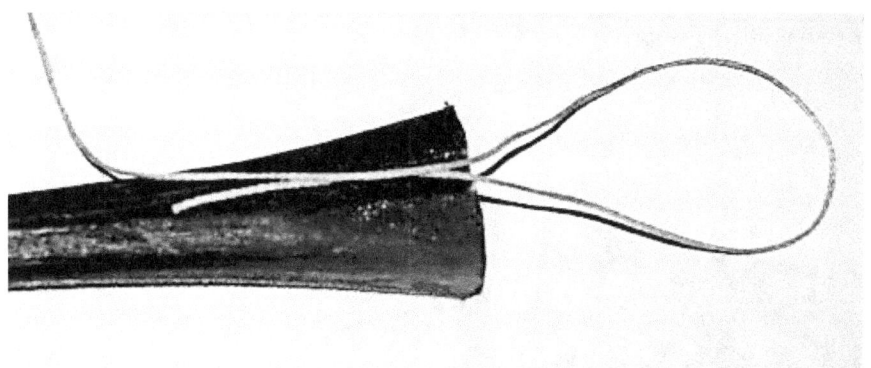

Take the long end of the cord and start winding it around the bill. Notice that the short tail is pulled off to the side at a diagonal. This is important, as it helps to lock the cord in:

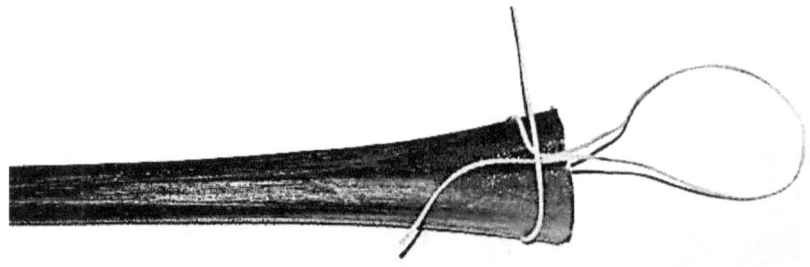

Keep wrapping for about two to three wraps toward the wide end of the bill, then stop:

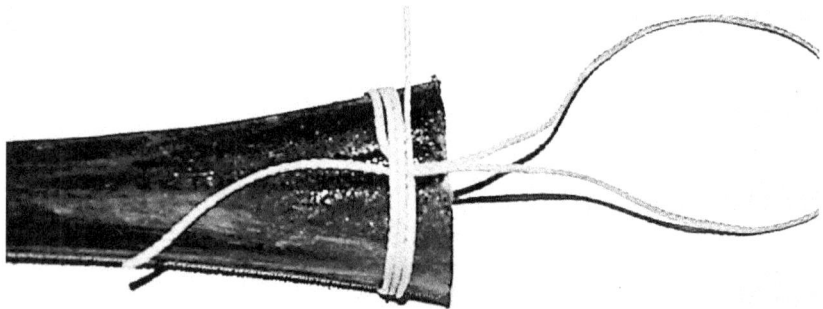

Now start wrapping back toward the skinny end of the bill, *over* the old wraps:

Keep wrapping down, making sure that the other end of the string is still off at an angle. Wrap all the way down, past the other end of the string, until you have enough of the bill wrapped to make a good hand-grip:

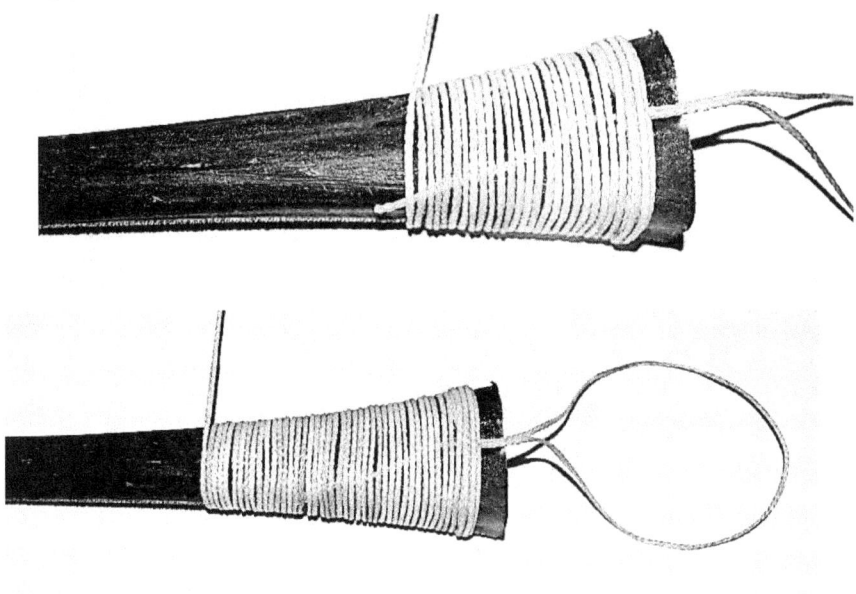

Next, turn the bill to the back side and lay down a small piece of dental floss or other fine cord on top of the wrap as shown below:

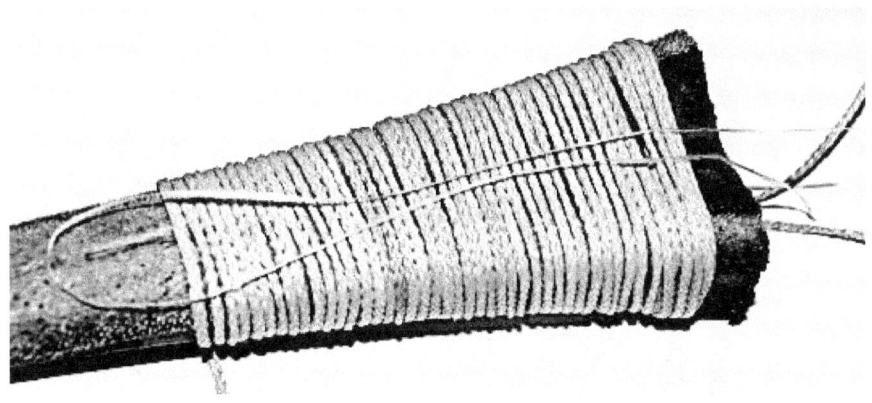

Now wrap the cord at least three times toward the narrow end of the bill and over the floss:

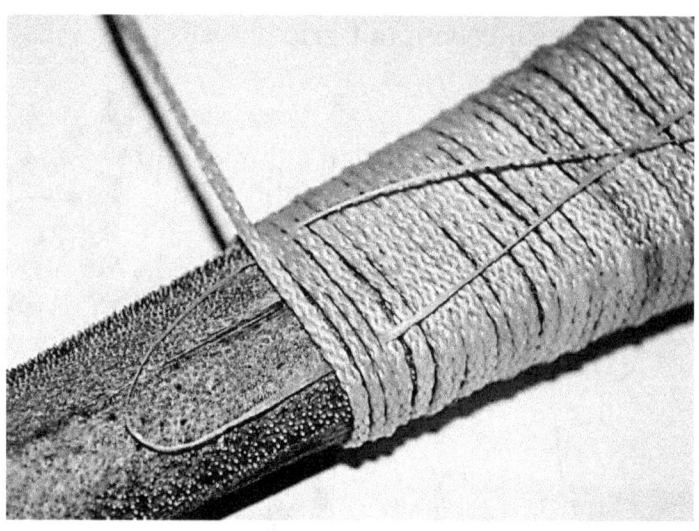

Next, cut the cord, leaving a two or three inch tail:

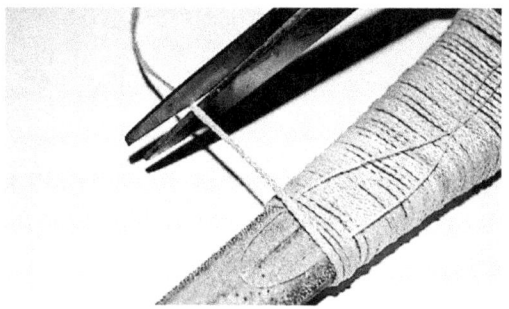

Thread the end of the cord through the dental floss loop:

Pull on the floss, pulling the cord partially under the wrap:

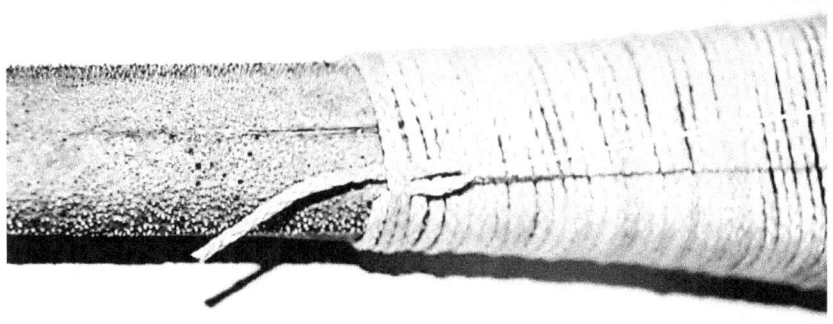

Now, use a small knife or scissors to cut the loop, leaving the end sticking out slightly:

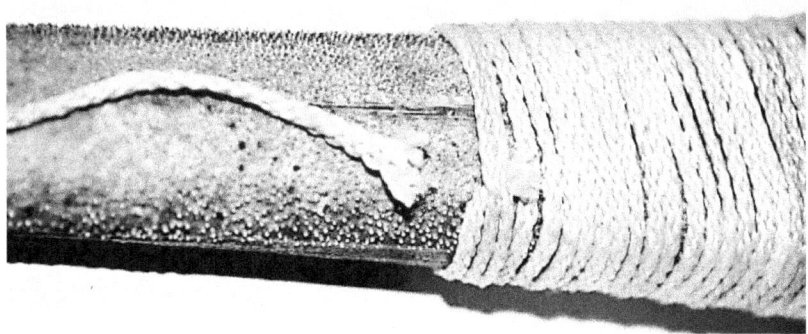

If you are using nylon cord, you can use a match to melt the tip. Otherwise, you can use a dab of hot glue or something else to keep the string in place. The finished dagger should look like this:

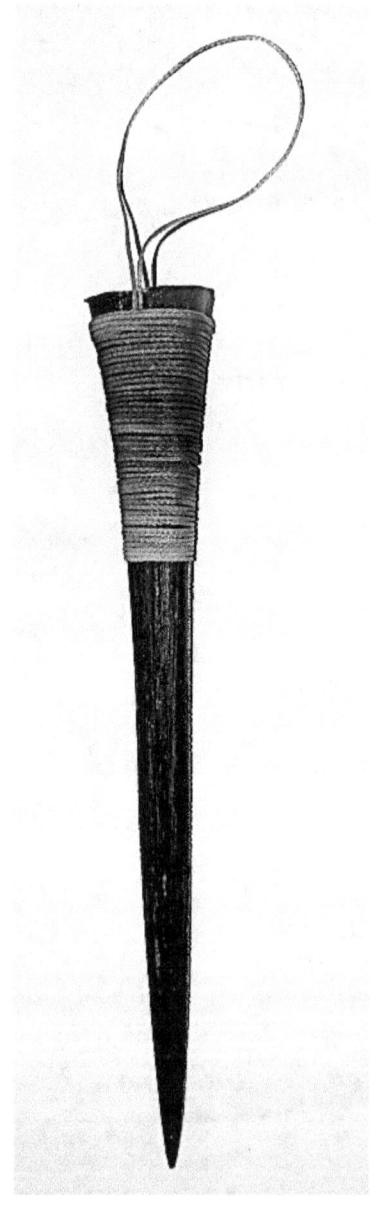

The Hawai'ian Hut

By Hope Mashburn

Hawai'i's pleasant climate helped determine the type of buildings that the early Hawai'ians lived in. Instead of building large heat-conserving dwellings to spend their days in, they built huts predominantly for storage or for shelter from rain.

Captain King, who sailed with Captain Cook, was one of the first Europeans to describe a Hawai'ian house:

"...their method of living together in small towns or villages, containing from about one hundred to two hundred houses, built pretty close together, without any order, and having a winding path leading through them. They are generally flanked, toward the sea, with loose detached walls, which probably are meant both for the purposes of shelter and defense. The figure of their houses has been already described. They are of different sizes, from eighteen feet by twelve, to forty-five by twenty-four. There are some of a larger kind; being fifty feet long and thirty broad, and quite open at one end. These, they told us, were designed for travelers or strangers, who were only making a short stay.

In addition to the furniture of their houses, which has been accurately described by Captain Cook, I have only to add, that at one end are mats on which they sleep, with wooden pillows, or sleeping stools, exactly like those of the Chinese. Some of the better sort of houses have a courtyard before them, neatly railed in, with smaller houses built round it, for their servants. In this area they generally eat, and sit during the daytime. In the sides of the hills, and among the steep rocks, we also observed several holes or caves, which appeared to be inhabited; but as the entrance was defended with wicker-work, and we also found, in the only one that was visited, a stone fence running across it within, we imagine they are principally designed for places of retreat, in case of an attack from an enemy."

The commoners tended to use their buildings to protect their food and possessions, and to sleep in during wet or cold weather. They spent the majority of their lives outdoors– sleeping, eating, and living. Each family would build their huts with their own hands and the help of a few friends. However, when the chief wanted a house, the commoners would prepare any of the materials needed and build the house for him. An architect would oversee the construction. The houses for the chiefs were larger, and the chiefs spent more time in their houses than the commoners did, both day and night.

The Hawai'ians built many different types of huts. A typical hut would consist of a small opening used as a door, often with no window openings. The doors and windows had no coverings; they were just left open. Often, the door was a hole only just big enough for a single person to crawl through. There were also huts that were completely open on either one or both ends.

Hawai'ians often used sweet-smelling pili grass for the thatched roofs of their huts. They tied the grass into bundles and then attached them to the support beams. They would use cordage made of natural materials to make ropes for the pili bundles. Three commonly used rope materials were coconut shell fiber, 'uki 'uki grass, or 'ie 'ie branches.

When pili grass was not readily available, the Hawai'ians used other local resources for their thatched roofs. Other roof materials were sugar cane leaves, banana trunk fibers, pandanus leaves, other grasses, or ti leaves.

Many Hawai'ian villages were located on shielded beaches to protect the people from bad weather and to be close to the ocean for fishing. Some Hawai'ians made temporary huts that were built in the more central section of the island which they used while they worked in 'uala (sweet potato) and taro fields. They also stayed in their temporary huts when they were going inland to collect some of the natural resources from the forests. Hawai'ians continued to build grass houses even into modern times.

Jesse Kunewa describes a hut that was once located on the beach where the headwall now stands in Kailua Kona (Kailua Bay):

"In the late 1930's and early 1940's my grandfather was the custodian for the Hulihee Palace and grounds. At that time there was a grass hut on the kau [south] side of the palace. When children came from other islands to stay at the palace, they slept in the grass shack. When I was a young boy, my sisters, brothers, and cousins stayed in the grass shack when we visited my grandfather. This grass shack was made out of pili grass. I remember it really kept the rain out!

I also remember around this same time that there was still a Hawai'ian village of huts being used at Kealakekua Bay in Captain Cook."

Examples of Hawai'ian Hut Designs

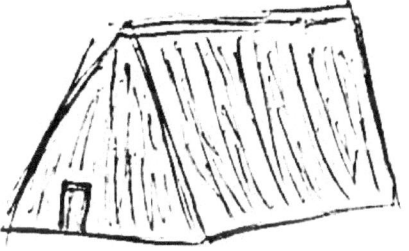

This hut's roof is built right down to the ground, with straight rafters.

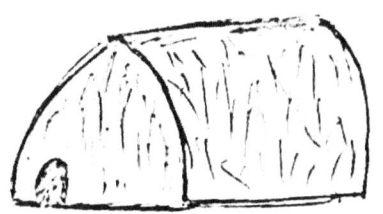

This hut's roof is also built down to the ground, except its rafters are curved.

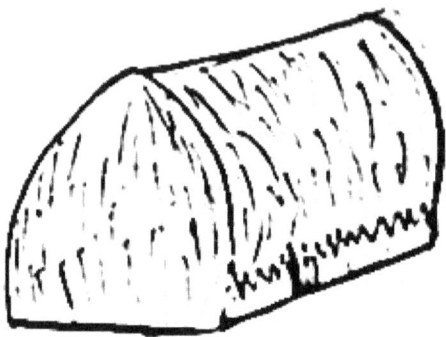

This hut is bigger than the previous examples. It has curved rafters that are set on walls.

This hut is also a larger style. It has straight rafters that are set on walls.

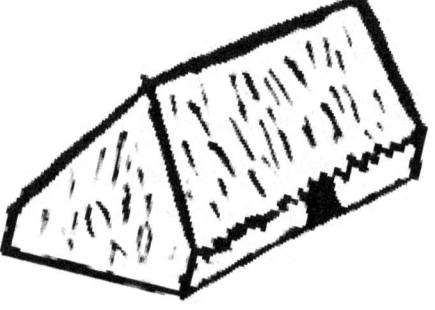

This hut was built with its roof propped up on top of short rock walls. The ends were left uncovered. Huts like these are still used today to store canoes.

How to Make a Shaka

One of the skills needed to build a Hawai'ian hut is to make a shaka. The shaka allows you to easily have access to a long length of rope without it getting tangled.

Start by putting the end of the cord between your thumb and in-dex finger, making sure the short end goes on the *inside* of your hand, not the outside (otherwise it won't work).

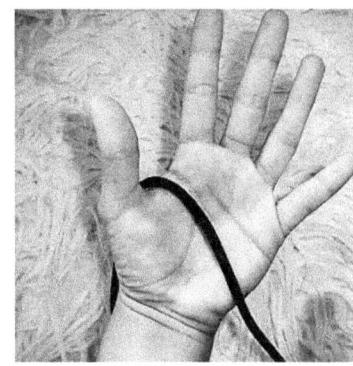

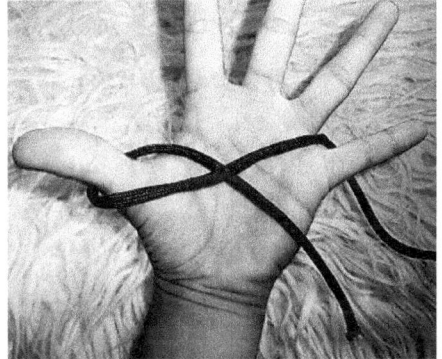

Then take the long end and pull it around your thumb and over your pinky, making sure to keep the dangling end free of the loops.

Pull the cord back over and around your thumb.

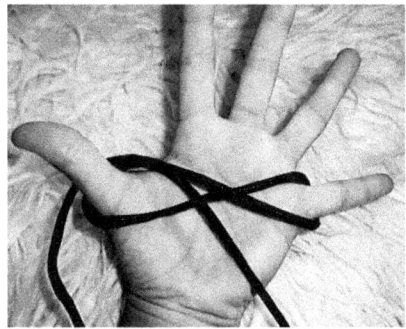

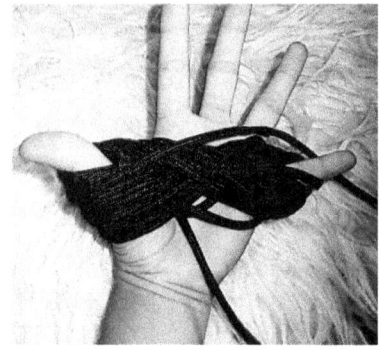

Keep wrapping the chord around your fingers, always following the same pattern. Make sure to try to keep your hand as stretched out as possible. Keep wrapping until you have about a foot and a half of extra chord left.

Pull the chord off of your thumb, and hold your half-made shaka in your hand, keeping the pinky in the bottom to make sure that it won't unravel.

Form a loop with the long end of the cord, pulling it over and tightening it around the rest of the cord. Do *not* make a knot—just wind the cord around the bundle. You will have to move your thumb out of the way to tighten it.

Pull it tight, and then wrap it again three to four times.

If you made your shaka correctly, you should be able to pull the end of your cord (the end that you *didn't* tie your loops with), and your cord should unravel with no knots. It may take a couple of tries to perfect it.

The Ukulele

By Teah Van Bergen

Ukulele. "uku" means fleas and "lele" means to jump. It is said that the Hawai'ians chose this odd name for the instrument because when they watched the Portuguese play it, their fingers were hopping all over the neck of the ukulele. However, Queen Lili'uokalani had a different interpretation of the word. She said that "ukulele" means the gift that came. Her interpretation was that "uku" means gift or reward, and "lele" means "to come from." This would make sense considering that the ukulele was a gift from the Portuguese. Portuguese immigrants brought the original instrument, called a machete de braca (or machete de braga), to Hawai'i in 1879. The ukulele was later developed from this instrument.

In late August of 1879, The Hawai'ian Gazette reported that the Portuguese delighted the Hawai'ians with nightly concerts. One of these immigrants was Manuel Nunues, who became one of the earliest ukulele makers in the world. He operated his Ukulele Manufacturing for forty years and passed down his ukulele constructing skills to many others. Since that time, the ukulele has become one of the most popular instruments in Hawai'i and is used in much Hawai'ian music today.

As you can see in the picture, the ukulele looks just like a mini guitar, but with four strings instead of six. There are four different sizes of ukuleles. In order from largest to smallest there is the baritone, tenner, concert, and soprano. The size that most people are familiar with is the concert.

There are three main sections to a ukulele.

The head is the part that holds the tuners and the neck is where you place your fingers to create a chord on the strings. The body is where you strum to create a sound. There are

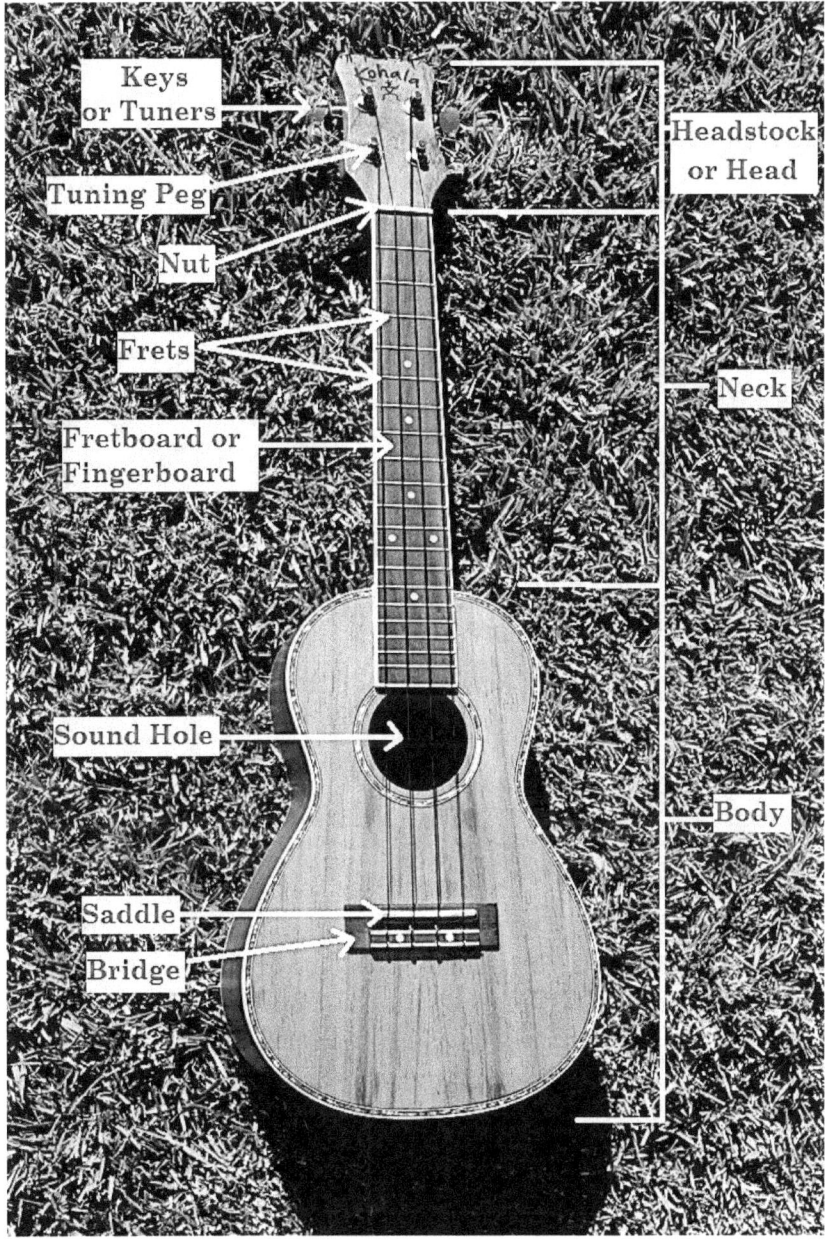

seventeen horizontal bars on the neck of the ukulele called frets. Whenever you are going to create a cord, you put your fingers on the strings and in between the frets. Each string has a letter to symbolize it. When you are properly holding a ukulele, the strings are labeled as G, C, E, and A. A is the highest-sounding string and G is the lowest.

When you are reading a song, the cords will be written above the words to show where in the song you switch to another cord. To play a ukulele, you place the fingers of your left hand (if you are right-handed) on the neck of the ukulele to create a chord:

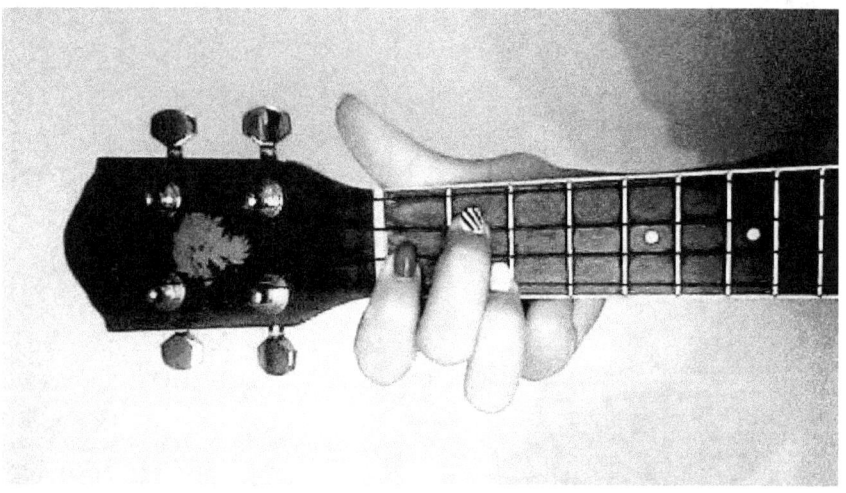

On the following page are some useful ukulele cords that you will find in many songs. The diagrams represent the fret board of the ukulele if it was standing upright and facing you. The top line represents the nut. The line on the far left represents the "G" string, and the line on the far right represents the "A" string. The dots show where your fingers go.

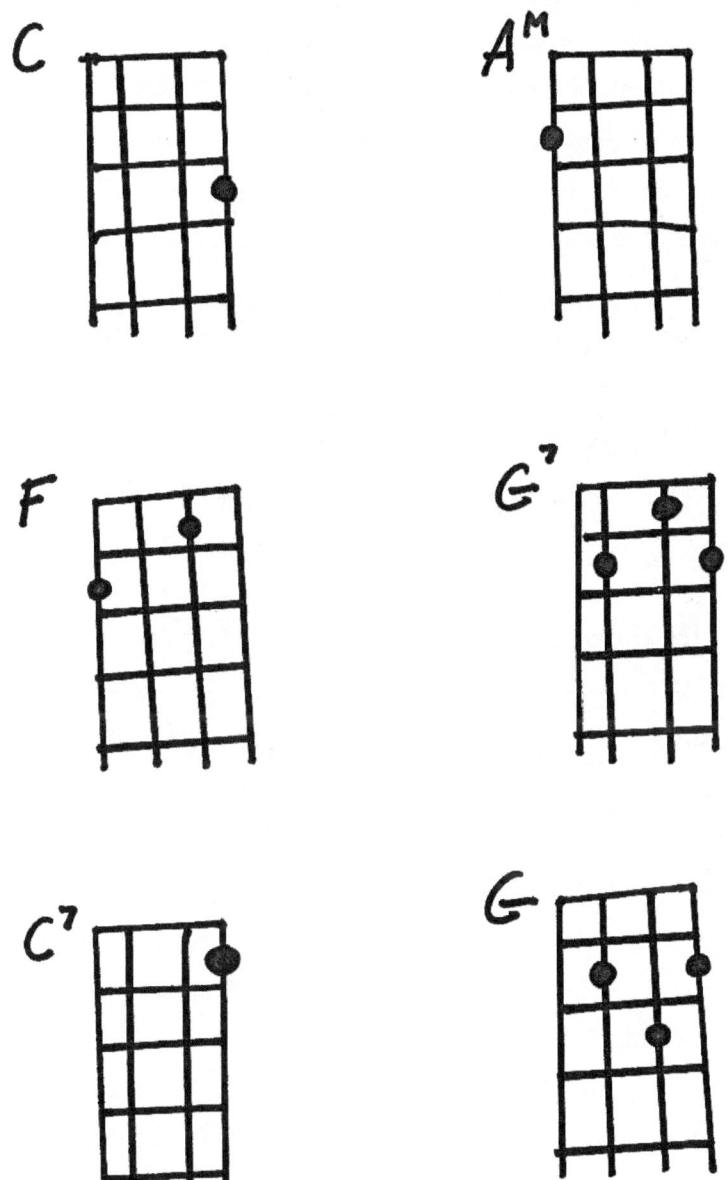

While you are forming cords with one hand, you take the other hand and brush it up and down against the strings to create a rhythm. Your fingers should strum either over the sound hole or closer to where the neck meets the body.

I strongly encourage you to go out and learn how to play the ukulele! It is a very rewarding experience.

Ni'ihau Shell Jewelry
By Molly Russell

Each Hawai'ian island has its own official flower, but the island of Ni'ihau chose a shell instead of a flower. The people of Ni'ihau are known for making gorgeous leis, not from flowers, but from shells. In 1778, Captain James Cook wrote about the beautiful shell leis made by the women of Ni'ihau. Many explorers and travelers since then have noted the beauty and variety of the Ni'ihau shells and jewelry. Ni'ihau shell jewelry can be seen in museums around the world.

Ni'ihau is seventeen miles southwest of Kaua'i across the Kaulakahi Channel. The land area is approximately 70 square miles. Once formed as a volcanic mountain millions of years ago, it has now eroded. The highest point is only about 1,280 feet and most of the island is less than 500 feet above sea level. The winter months have rough seas and windy weather that wash ashore the famous shells of Ni'ihau. High mountains on its close neighbor, Kaua'i, keep clouds from reaching Ni'ihau so there is not much rain. The climate is dry and often has droughts.

In 1864, the Sinclair family, originally from Scotland, came to Hawai'i from New Zealand. They were looking to purchase land for ranching. King Kamehameha IV sold Ni'ihau to the Sinclair family for $10,000. The family took over ownership of the island which came with the responsibility to care for the island as an ali'i (chief) would. They created a cattle and sheep ranch and employed the people of Ni'ihau. They later added bee keeping and charcoal production to the economy, though now most of these employment opportunities are gone.

Sinclair family descendants still own Ni'ihau, although now under the name Robinson. In order to visit the island today people must first ask the Robinsons for permission.

The Robinsons have helped promote the shell leis of Ni'ihau by selling them in gift shops on neighboring islands. Ni'ihau shell jewelry and leis are so special that in 2004 the governor of Hawai'i signed a law that says that no one can claim that they are selling Ni'ihau shell jewelry unless the shells are mostly from the island of Ni'ihau and the jewelry is completely made in the state of Hawai'i.

Momi Shells

There are three main types of shells used in Ni'ihau leis. The momi shell has an oval shape and is about 10mm long. The word momi means "pearl." There are over twenty different color variations of momi shells. The darker colored shells are rarer than the lighter colored ones.

Kaheleani Shell

Another type of shell is the kahelelani shell. It is a small turban shaped shell 3-5mm in size. The kahelelani is the smallest of the Ni'ihau shells and the most expensive. The colors range from light pink to brown and black. It is the most tedious to collect because it is so small.

The third type of shell most common in Ni'ihau shell jewelry is the laiki shell. Its name means "rice," and it is the size and shape of a grain of rice. Its color can range from white to yellow and it is used in the traditional Ni'ihau wedding lei.

Laiki Shells

The process of making Ni'ihau jewelry is not complicated, but it is very time consuming. It begins in the winter when the Ni'ihau women and children walk down to the beaches to collect the shells. On a good day they can fill a sixteen-ounce jar, but on an average day they will only fill a small baby food jar. The women lie on their stomachs so they can see the shells more clearly. The work is usually very hot and slow.

Older women will stay home to sort, pierce, and string the shells. They sort the shells into piles according to color, size, and type, discarding any that are cracked or damaged. They only use about ten percent of the shells they collect.

How to Make Shell Jewelry

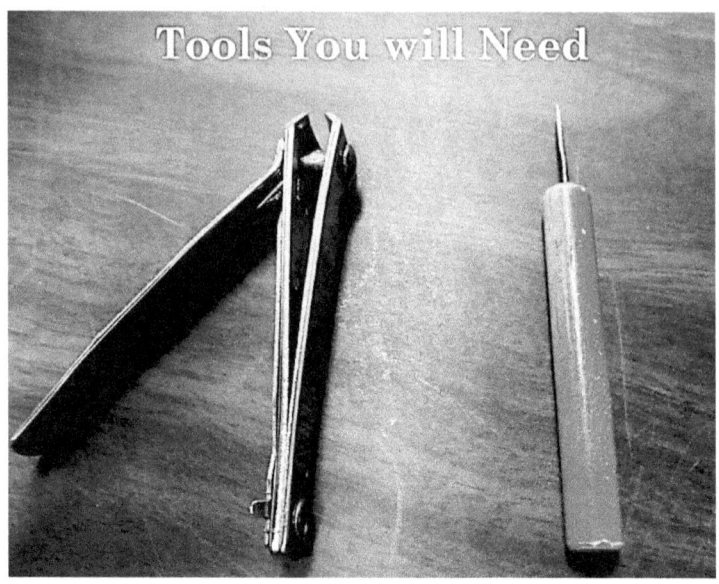

In order to drill the holes in the shells, first snip off the top cap of the shell with nail clippers:

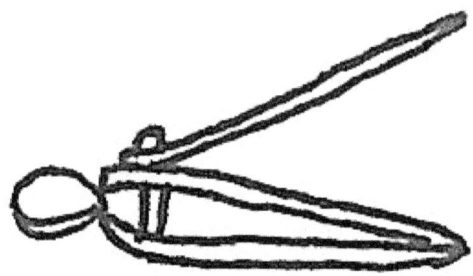

Then insert a fine metal point into the hole to make another tiny hole in the side of the shell. The location of the second hole determines how the shells will hang on the string. A pikake-style lei has shells fanning out from the center. A poepoe-style lei, sometimes called a rope style, is a rounded lei with the shells lying flat. It is the position of the hole that determines how the shells lie when strung.

Pikake Style

Poepoe Style

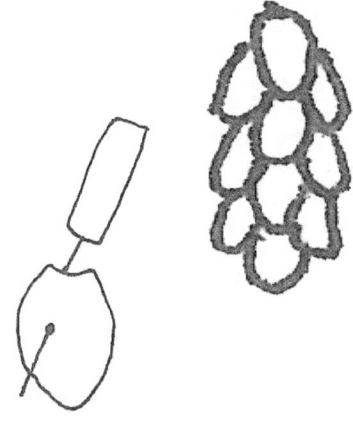

Once you have the holes in the shells, the next step is to count out the shells and sort them from largest to smallest. For earrings, you need thirty-two shells split into four groups of eight shells each. Take each group of shells and arrange it into a line with the largest shells at the bottom. One pair of lines will be for one earring and the other pair will be for the second earring.

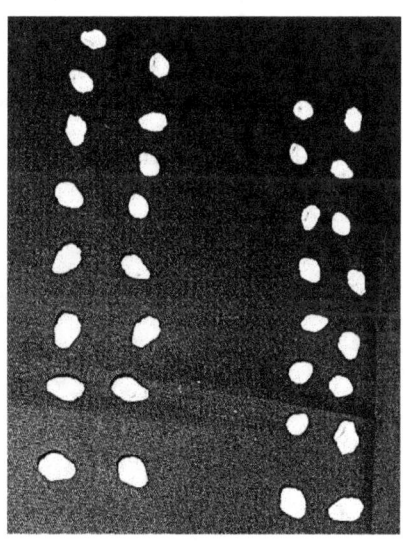

Arrangement for Earrings

Use a waxed linen thread to string the shells. The wax makes the end of the thread stiff and straight so it is easy to thread. The wax also holds the knots in place. The early Hawai'ians used coconut fibers for thread.

Thread the two largest shells from one pair of lines onto the middle of the thread. The thread in the photo below goes into the top hole in one shell, comes out the side hole of the same shell, goes into the side hole of the next shell, and out the top hole of the next shell. Once that is done, tie a tight overhand knot. Be sure to put the right-hand side thread over the left-hand side thread when tying knots to keep them consistent.

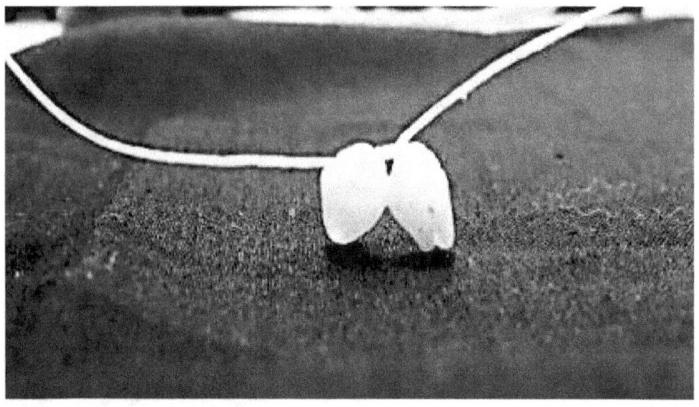

Next, thread the next two largest shells from the same pair of lines, one on each side, and tie another overhand knot. Note the placement of the shells below:

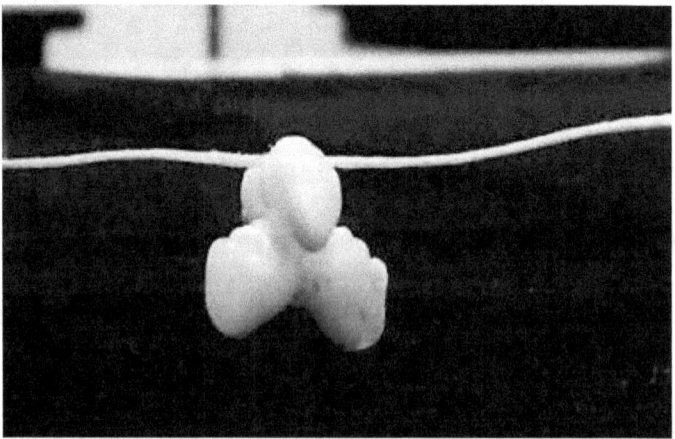

Keep repeating these steps as you work your way up the lines of shells until you have put all of them on the thread:

The next step is to tie off the earring with a small puka shell. A puka shell is the top of a cone shell with a hole eroded in it. Puka means hole in Hawai'ian.

Puka Shells

Slide one thread through the puka shell, then through a small metal ring, and back through the puka shell:

Tie a double knot with the threads and cut off the extra. Attach a wire earring hook to the ring. Repeat for the second earring.

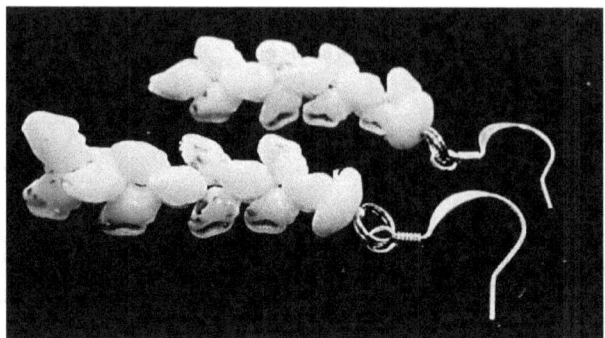

The number of shells for a bracelet or lei will depend on how long you want to make it. Once you have determined your size, split your shells into two equal groups. Arrange each group into two equal lines of shells with the largest shell in the middle of each line, and the other shells getting progressively smaller as they get farther from the middle.

To start a bracelet or lei, use two long pieces of thread and loop them together. This creates two sides with the loop being the center of the bracelet or lei. String shells on the two sides separately, starting with the largest shells in the middle:

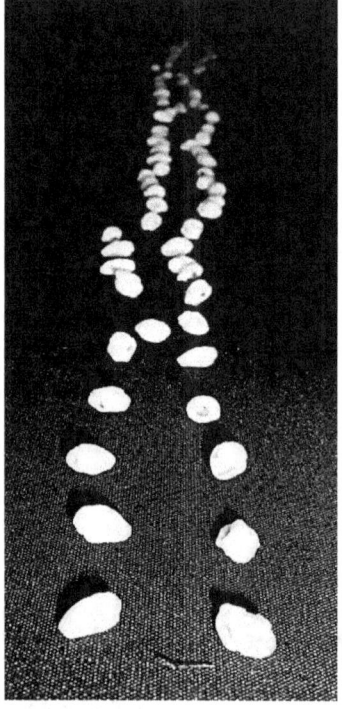

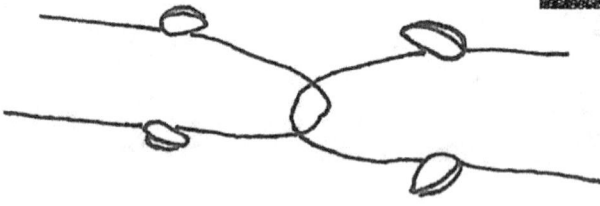

Thread and tie the knots the same as the earrings. Repeat this process until all of the shells are used, or until it reaches the length that you want.

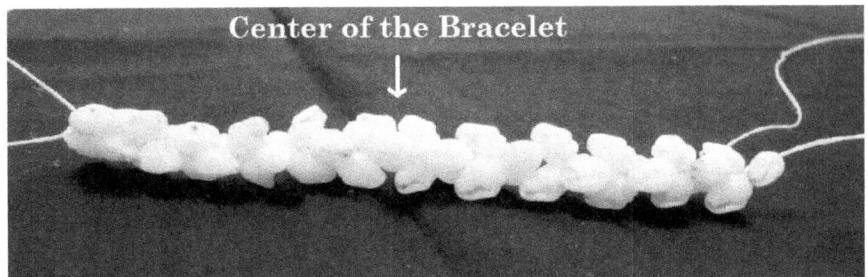

Tie the ends off with a puka shell just like with the earrings, but use a bigger shell and, instead of an earring hook, attach a clasp.

Making a Lauhala Bracelet
By Charlee Brown

Leaves from the hala tree, called lauhala, were often used by the ancient Hawai'ians for weaving. They can vary from two to five feet in length.

Hala Tree

Lauhala can be woven into hats, bracelets, and mats. In the past they were used for covering huts and making sails for canoes. Scientists have found remains of lauhala and things woven from them in ancient caves, showing that the Hawai'ians have used lauhala for many years.

How to Make a Lauhala Bracelet

To make a lauhala bracelet all you need is one lauhala leaf and a pair of scissors or clippers to cut it off the tree.

Find a hala tree, take your scissors or clippers, go to the very back of a leaf and snip it. Cut one leaf for each bracelet you want to make. The thicker leaves are easier to weave, but the thinner ones make a more delicate bracelet.

Snip off the ends of the lauhala leaf and trim the sides so that it forms an even strip. Then, put it out in the sun to dry. Make sure that it dries to the point where it won't rot, but is still flexible to work with.

Next, take your dried hala leaf and wet it a bit so that it doesn't crack while weaving. Then, straighten it out, making it look like one long strip:

Next, wrap it *twice* around your knuckles:

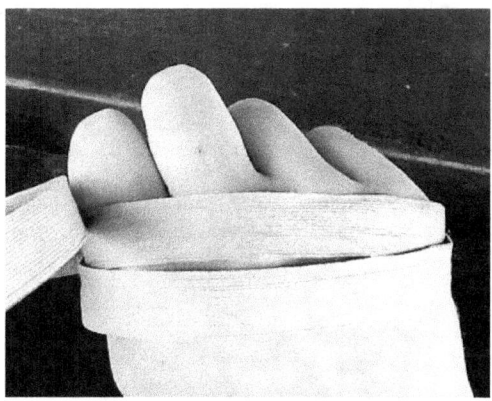

Hold the loop with your free hand, and slip your other hand out of the loop:

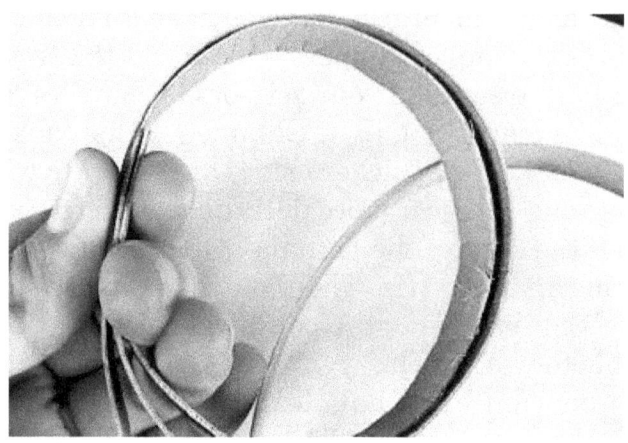

Now it's time to start weaving. Hold the loop so that the long tail is on the top. Then, take the tail on the top of the loop and fold it to the left as shown in the photo below. Make sure that the piece going off to the side is perpendicular to the rest of the loop. For this fold, and all of the following folds, crease the leaves as you go to help them stay in place:

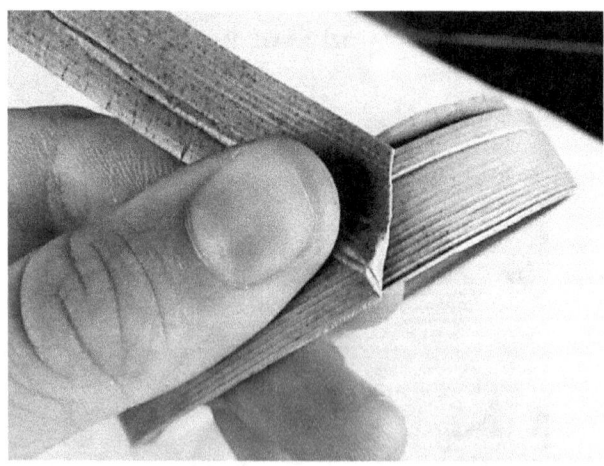

Now, take the free end and pull it through the loop:

Next, fold the tail straight up:

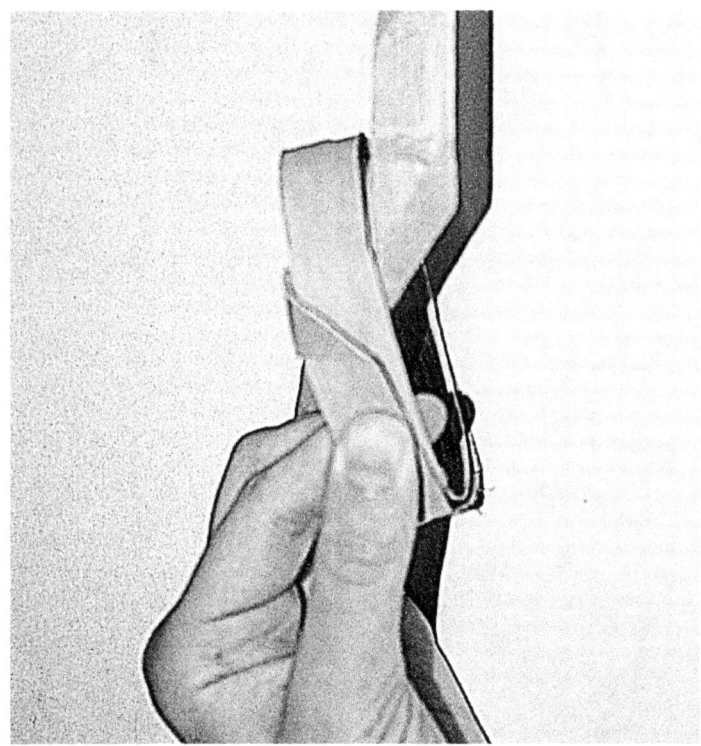

Flip the folded piece up on to the loop:

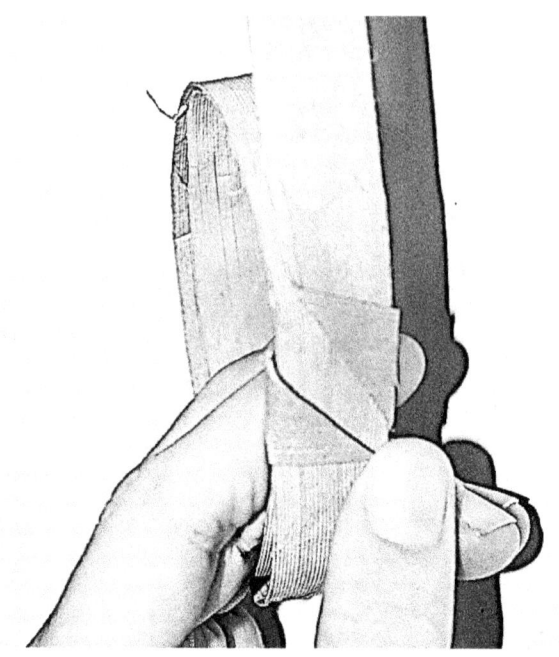

Now, fold it to the left, just like the very first fold you made:

Fold the free end through the loop again:

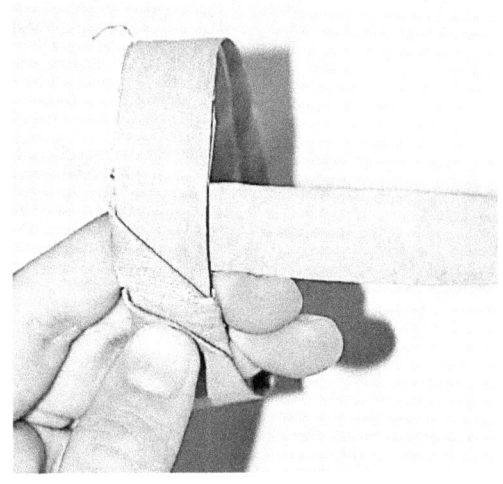

Fold the tail straight up:

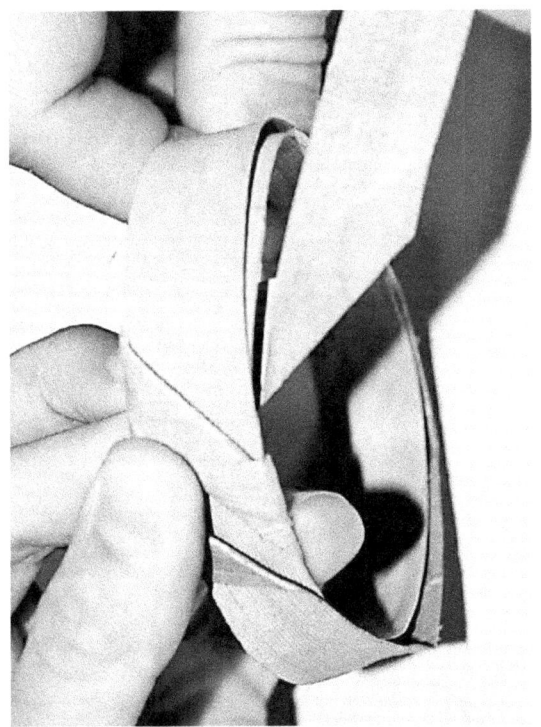

Flip the folded piece on to the loop just like you did before. Keep repeating the steps until you have gone all around the loop. Make sure you are pulling it tight every once in a while or else it will become bumpy.

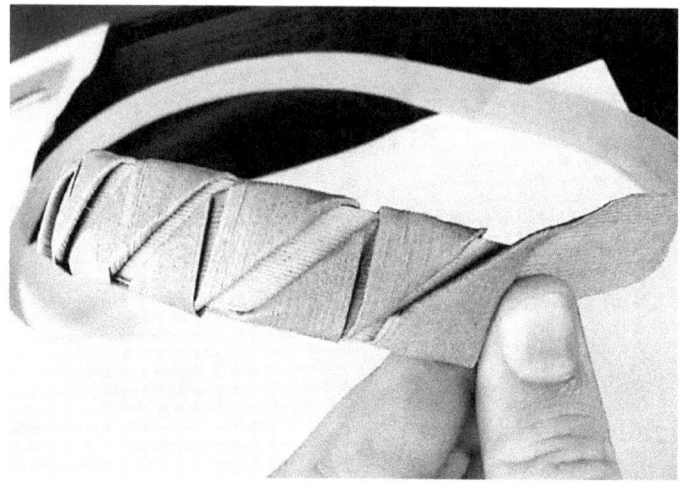

When you get to the end of the loop, pull the free end through the loop and cut it so that there are about three inches left hanging:

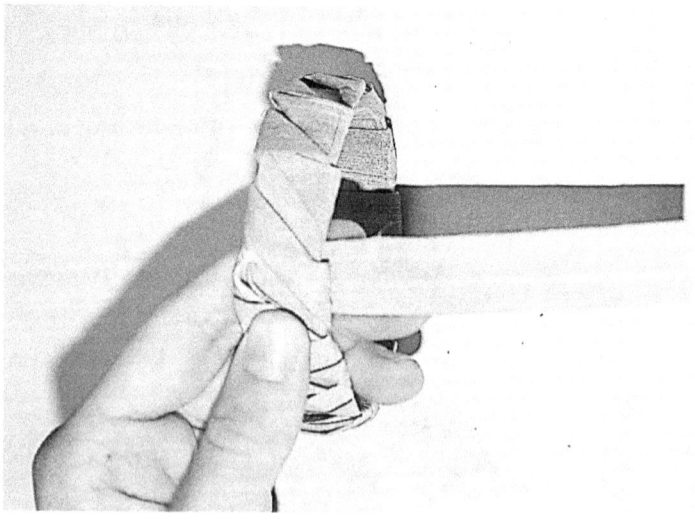

Now, fold it straight up, just like in the previous steps:

Flip it up on to the loop, just like in the previous steps:

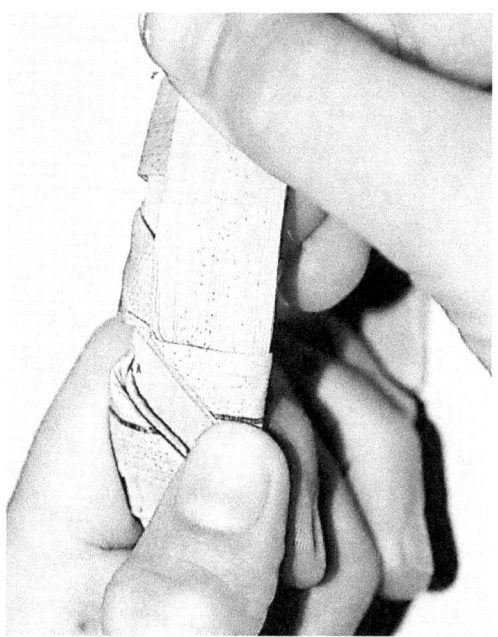

Fold it to the left, the same as your very first fold:

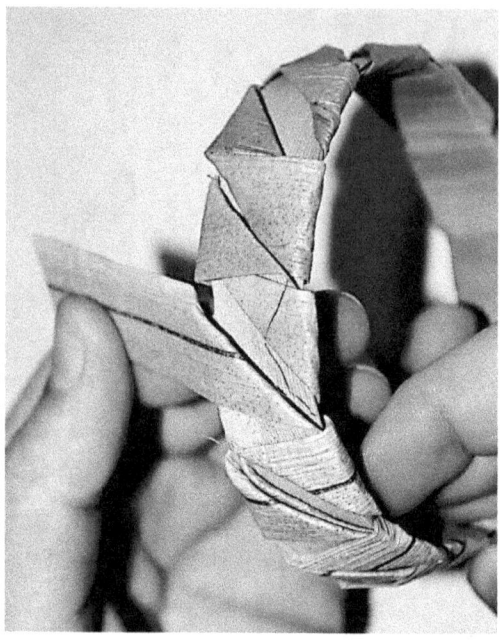

Fold it through the loop one last time, and tuck it behind one of the folds *inside* of the bracelet:

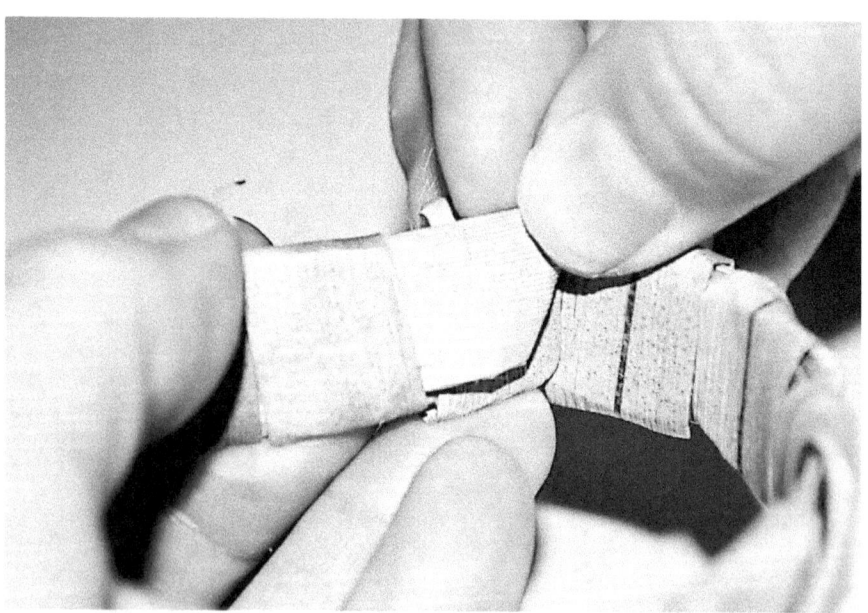

Here is what it should look like after you have tucked it completely under:

Your bracelet is now finished. Make sure you don't get it wet. When you are going to the beach, taking a shower, or even washing your hands, be sure to take the bracelet off.

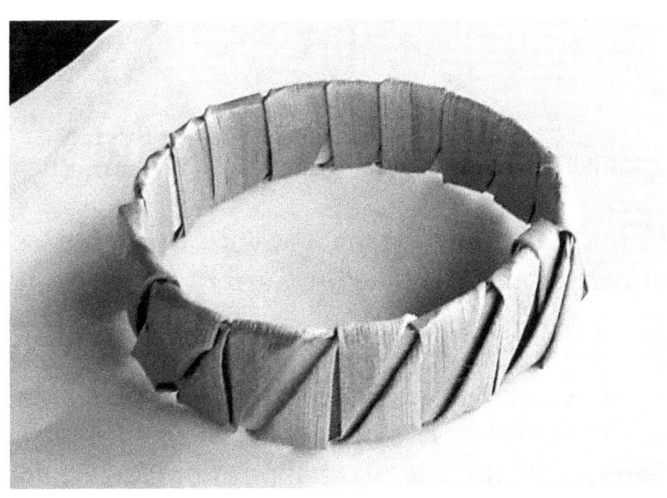

Enjoy your new lauhala bracelet!

He'e Nalu (Surfing)
By Teah Van Bergen

The waves are enticing, the ocean is pono, and the kukui nut polished boards just dried; let's go he'e nalu! In the 1700s a new sport called he'e nalu was introduced to the world. You may be familiar with this sport, although you probably don't know it as he'e nalu, but as surfing.

Sketch of Early Hawai'ian Surfers
From ***Polynesian Researches*** **by William Ellis, 1831**

Captain King, who traveled with Captain Cook, recorded his impressions of Hawai'ian surfers in the 1700s:

Swimming is not only a necessary art, in which both their men and women are more expert than any people we had hitherto seen, but a favorite diversion amongst them. One particular mode, in which they sometimes amused themselves with this exercise, in Karakakooa Bay, appeared to us most perilous and extraordinary, and well deserving a distinct relation.

The surf, which breaks on the coast round the bay, extends to the distance of about one hundred and fifty yards from the shore, within which space, the surges of the sea, accumulating from the shallowness of the water, are dashed against the beach with prodigious violence. Whenever, from stormy weather, or any extraordinary swell at sea, the impetuosity of the surf is increased to its utmost height, they choose that time for this amusement, which is performed in the following manner: twenty or thirty of the natives, taking each a long narrow board, rounded at the ends, set out together from the shore. The first wave they meet, they plunge under, and suffering it to roll over them, rise again beyond it, and make the best of their way; by swimming out into the sea. The second wave is encountered in the same manner with the first; the great difficulty consisting in seizing the proper moment of diving under it, which, if missed, the person is caught by the surf, and driven back again with great violence; and all his dexterity is then required to prevent himself from being dashed against the rocks. As soon as they have gained, by these repeated efforts, the smooth water beyond the surf, they lay themselves at length on their board, and prepare for their return. As the surf consists of a number of waves, of which every third is remarked to be always much larger than the others, and to flow higher on the shore, the rest breaking in the intermediate space, their first object is to place themselves on the summit of the largest surge, by which they are driven along with amazing rapidity toward the shore. If by mistake they should place themselves on one of the smaller waves, which breaks before they reach the land, or should not be able to keep their plank in a proper direction on the top of the swell, they are left exposed to the fury of the next, and, to avoid it, are obliged again to dive, and regain the place from which they set out. Those who succeed in their object of reaching the shore, have still the greatest danger to encounter. The coast being guarded by a chain of rocks, with, here and there, a small opening between them, they are obliged to steer their board through one of these, or, in case of failure, to quit it, before they reach the rocks,

*and, plunging under the wave, make the best of their way back
again. This is reckoned very disgraceful, and is also attended
by the loss of the board, which I have often seen, with great
terror, dashed to pieces, at the very moment the islander quit-
ted it. The boldness and address, with which we saw them perform these difficult and dangerous maneuvers, was all together astonishing and is scarcely to be credited.*

The Hawai'ians had their own recordings of he'e nalu. Ancient petroglyphs have been found that show images of surfers.

Surfing was more than just a fun activity for the early
Hawai'ians. It was also used in spiritual rituals, exercise, and
the settlement of conflicts. Many spiritual events surrounded
surfing, whether it was praying for good surf, building a
board, or rituals for just the art of riding a wave. Surfing was
used by the ali'i (chiefs) as a strengthening exercise. Surfing
could also be used to resolve conflict. A bet would be made
and surfing could determine the winner. However, the early
Hawai'ians loved surfing, so it was mainly done for pure
pleasure.

The early Hawai'ians were also very skilled craftsmen. To
make a surf board the craftsman would shape a log, often
made from koa wood, with an adz. Next, he would rub it with
coral to smooth out the cut marks, and then sand it with pum-
ice stone or various grades of sand. For a final polish he might
have used water and sharkskin. Sometimes the boards were
stained with various plant dyes or charred kukui nuts. Once
the board was complete, he would apply a coat of kukui nut
oil.

Surfing has evolved through the years. Instead of long
heavy wooden boards, most people these days use light, foam
boards. The more advanced surfers use short fiberglass
boards. There are now various types of boards from all over
the world.

The most well-known surfer of his time was Duke Kahanamoku (1890-1968). He had many nicknames, and was some-

times called "The Father of Surfing." Duke Kahanamoku was one of the people who introduced surfing to the rest of the modern world. His passion for surfing was deep, and he loved the ocean. He was also a five-time Olympic medalist in swimming. He is one of the reasons why surfing became popular worldwide.

Surfing has changed throughout the years, but what hasn't changed is the passion and competitions. Many surfing competitions are held today–they just have more modern prizes.

How to Surf

There are many different boards, but the most common ones are long or short fiberglass boards, or foam boards. Short boards are for people who are more advanced surfers, and long boards are for beginners. Beginners should use the type of board displayed below.

Before you even get into the water, you need to prepare your board. When you're using a fiberglass short or long board, you need to wax your board really well. If you have a foam board, waxing is not necessary, unless you want to. You can find surf board wax in any surf shop.

While you are actually surfing, you must have your leash on at all times. The leash is attached from the board to your ankle and helps keep the board from floating away if you fall off it. If you're right footed, then you would normally put your leash on your right foot and vice versa. Just remember that your leash goes on whatever foot is behind you when you stand up on a wave.

First, lay down flat on your board:

Start paddling with your hands cupped:

Sit on your board as shown while waiting for a wave:

When you see a wave, start paddling really hard:

When you feel the surge of the wave, pop up as fast as you can. If you have trouble slowly go to your knees:

Then get up on one knee:

Quickly advance to both feet:

Then, stand up completely with your knees bent and your arms out for balance:

It is ok to catch the white wash:

Surfing is now a sport that thousands of people enjoy around the world. Next time you go surfing, think of the ancient Hawai'ians surfing with their heavy wooden boards. You are connected to them by your love of the surf.

Kapa Making and Dyeing

By Emily Risley

The early Hawai'ians wore clothing made out of pounded bark, called kapa. Its manufacturing process was long and difficult, so when an easier method of getting clothing came to the islands from the European and American traders, the number of kapa makers began to decline rapidly. Now there are very few left.

Making Kapa Cloth

Kapa is made from the inner bark of the *waoke* (also called the *wauke*), or paper mulberry.

Waoke was one of the plants brought to the islands by canoe, and it was carefully cultivated. After the Hawai'ians planted it, they would wait about one to two years, until it was slightly wider than a broom stick. Then they would cut down the stalk close to the base. Waukes send out runners that grow new trees, so the plant could grow new trees even after a stalk was cut. After harvesting (while the stalk was still green), the bark would be slit along the length of the stalk, from top to bottom, and peeled off.

The outer bark, both the brown and green layers, would be scraped off, leaving only the white inner bark, called bast.

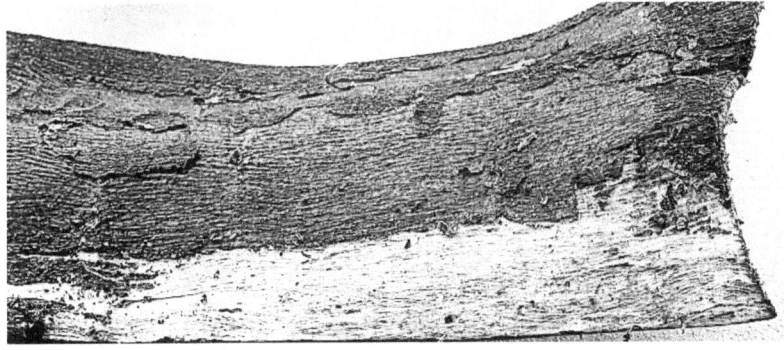

The bast strips were then rolled up in ti leaves and left to ferment in seawater for about a week. Fermentation allowed the fibers to spread out, yet still stick together. A good kapa maker could tell when the bast was done fermenting by the smell and feel of it.

After fermentation came the beating of the kapa. The bast was first pounded on a flat stone with a *hohoa* beater, which was a rounded club.

Then the kapa would be beat again, this time on a wooden anvil and with a different beater, one with four sides. The *pepehi* side of the beater would be used first. The *pepehi* side had many ridges in it, and made a deep pattern in the bark. Next would be the *ho'opa'i* side, which also had ridges, but they were smaller and mashed the fibers flatter. The final stage was called ho'oki. The beater used for this stage had a geometric design that was beaten into the cloth and formed a design like a watermark.

Kapa beaters
Photos Courtesy of the King Kamehameha Hotel in Kona, HI

The kapa would be moved back and forth over the wooden anvil with sticks, although some modern kapa makers now beat their kapa on a sheet of plastic which can be slid easily over the anvil.

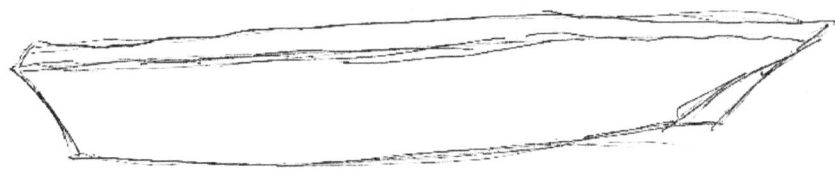

Wooden Kapa Anvil

Bast that Has Been Beaten Lying on a Wooden Anvil

To finish, the cloth would be left to dry in the sun.

Kapa Dye

Once the Hawai'ians had finished letting the kapa dry, it was ready to dye, though sometimes they dyed the bast before beating it. Kapa dyes were made from a variety of plants, which produced different colors. Here are some plants and the colors that can be made from them:

'Olena (turmeric): yellow
Noni bark: red
Noni root: yellow
Kukui nut shell: black
Kukui root: black
'Akala (native raspberry): pink
Pala'ā (lace fern): brownish red

Making the Dye
Materials

One of the plants above
Pounder (to crush the plant)
Bowl (to collect the juices)
Pot (for boiling)
Stirring spoon
Salt

First, cut the plant material up and crush it thoroughly. Then, put it into a pot along with water. The amounts you use will depend on the size of the cloth you want to dye. If the material you are using is from leaves, flowers, or fruits, do not heat it up, just mix in the water and then strain out the plant material to make the dye bath.

If the material you are using is from roots or bark, then after you have mixed the material with water, you will need to heat it up. If you are using powdered 'olena, use four tablespoons to one cup of water. Then place the pot on the stove at medium heat. The ancient Hawai'ians dropped in hot stones to heat the liquid, but using a stove is much easier. As the mixture starts to warm, stir repeatedly.

Bring the liquid to a boil for roots and bark, or boil it for five minutes if you are using 'olena powder. Then, remove the pot from the burner. Strain the mixture immediately.

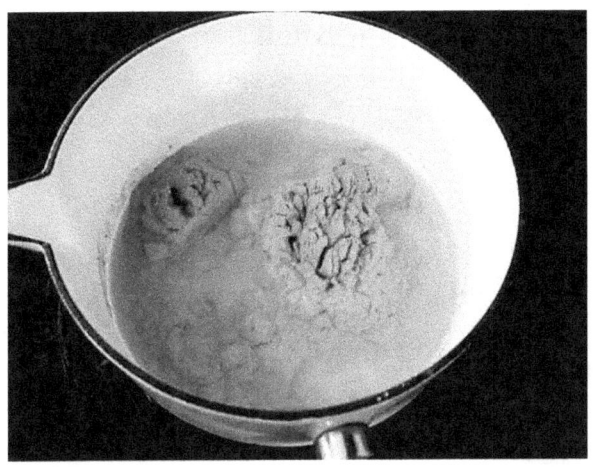

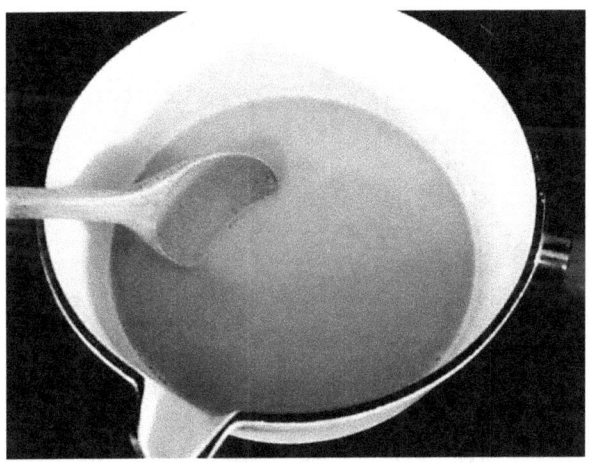

The early Hawai'ians used salt or urine to fix the dye to the cloth. One way to do this is to place the cloth in the dye bath for a few minutes and then add the salt. Use about one cup of salt for every three gallons of dye or one teaspoon for every cup. The salt not only helps the dye stick to the cloth, it will also make the dye darker.

Once you have dyed the cloth to the color that you like, remove it from the dye bath and gently wring it out. Hang it to air dry. If a darker color is needed, you can repeat the process with the same piece of fabric.

The dye may not last very long, so if you do not use it right away, store it in the refrigerator.

Kapa Printing

The early Hawai'ians not only decorated their kapa by dyeing it, they also printed or painted designs on it. Paintbrushes were mostly used for straight lines, but a bamboo stamp could have an intricate design which could be repeated over and over perfectly. Bamboo stamps were strips of bamboo with a pattern cut into them.

Bamboo Stamps for Printing Kapa

Printing the Cloth
Materials

One piece of kapa cloth
Dye
Stiff paint brush
Bamboo stamp (optional)

If you wish to paint the cloth, take the brush, dip it in the dye, and then *lightly* swipe it over the cloth. The idea is for the markings to show up clearly on one side, while the other side is blank. Before paintbrushes, the Hawai'ians used a folded piece of kapa dipped in dye, or seeds from the hala tree which are like little brushes.

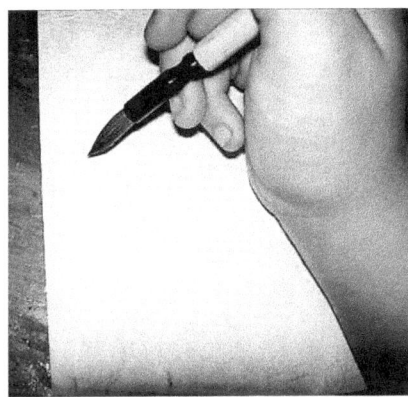 

If you wish to stamp the cloth, spread the dye over the bamboo stamp with the brush, and then carefully stamp the cloth. Repeat as desired. Usually, the same stamp is used over and over.

Quilting in Hawai'i

By Pearl Dickson

When the missionaries came to the Hawai'ian islands in the 1800s, they not only brought their faith to the islands, they also brought the art of quilting. However, Hawai'ian quilts have very different patterns from American or European quilts.

One folktale says that the Hawai'ian quilt patterns started with a Hawai'ian woman who had some cloth hanging on a clothesline. When she saw the sun fall on the cloth in a beautiful snowflake-like pattern, she got the idea for a quilt. Another tradition is that the missionaries taught the Hawai'ians how to cut paper snowflakes, and the Hawai'ians came up with the idea of using the same method to cut flower designs from cloth to applique on their quilts.

As time went on, mothers and grandmothers passed on the Hawai'ian quilting methods and patterns, which continues to this day. Men quilt too, and there is often at least one man in every quilt club.

How to Lay Out a Hawai'ian Quilting Square

1) First, pick a fabric for your background and a fabric for your pattern design. The two pieces of fabric should be the same size, and they should both be square. Wash the fabric before you start working with it to make sure that the dyes won't run and that they won't shrink after your project is complete.

2) Once you have prepared your fabric, you will need to iron the pieces in a special way. First, iron both pieces flat.

3) Next, take each piece and fold it in half. Note that the fold is on the bottom edge:

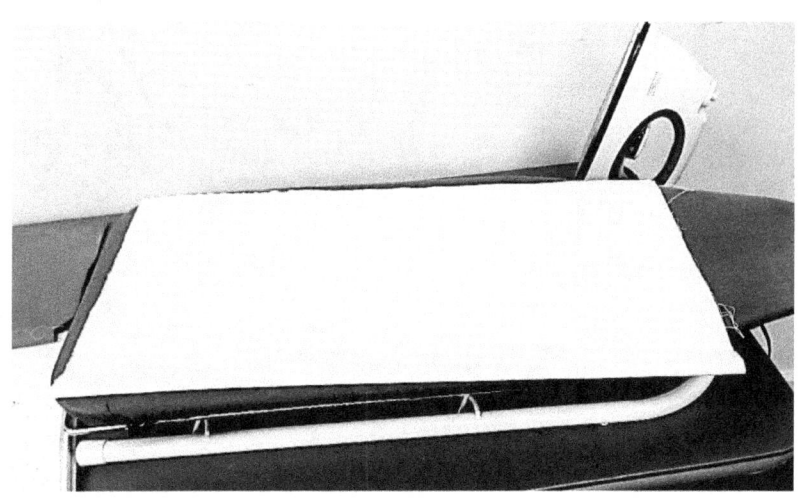

4) Then fold it right to left:

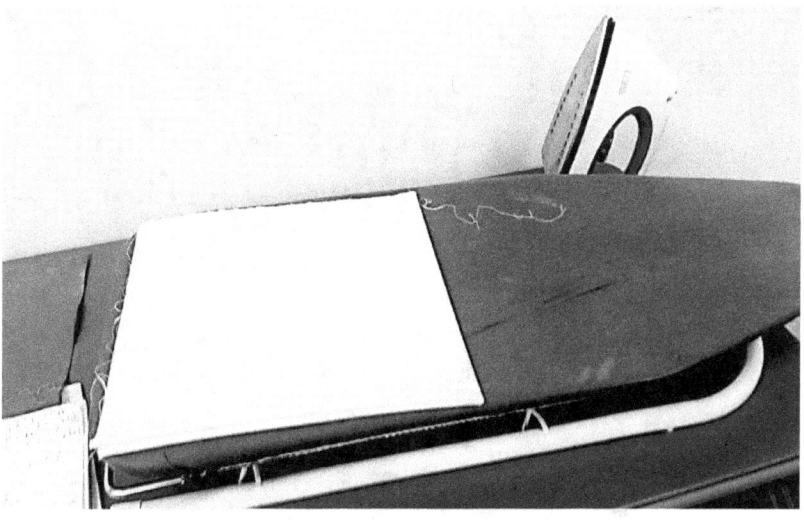

5) Next, with the fold still on the bottom, take the top right corner and pull it down to the bottom left corner:

6) Iron it. Do this with *both* pieces of fabric. Don't worry if your pattern fabric does not fold perfectly and ends up looking like the picture below, it will still work:

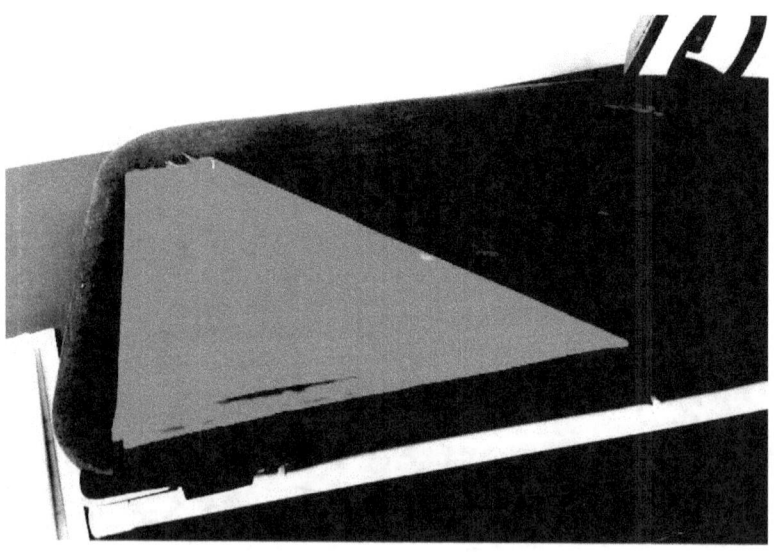

7) Line the fabric up so it looks like the photo below. The bottom point in the photo below is the same point as the one at the bottom right of the photo in step 6:

8) Cut your pattern out of a piece of paper:

9) Lay the pattern on your fabric and draw the outline on to the fabric:

10) Cut your pattern out of the fabric:

11) Open your design up and place it on your background fabric, using the ironing lines as guides. If you ironed the two pieces of fabric properly, the ironing lines should match up:

Your Hawai'ian quilting pattern is now ready to quilt!

Preparing for a Hawai'ian Lu'au
By Hope Mashburn

In this article I'm going to explain how to make some of the dishes that can be found at a Hawai'ian lu'au. Lu'aus are Hawai'ian parties that often have entertainment such as hula. Modern-day lu'aus contain traditional Hawai'ian foods along with foods from the countries of the immigrants to Hawai'i.

Kalua pig is the main dish at a lu'au; it's almost always served. Traditionally the Hawai'ians cooked pigs in a pit called an imu. An imu is a giant pit that you dig in the ground and then pile high with wood, tea leaves, and other things to cook your pork inside of.

Kalua Pig

Ingredients

Rocks—it is very important to use rocks that are covered in holes. Do *not* use smooth stones, or they will explode. It is also important not to use rocks with any salt or water in them.
Pork butt
Old newspaper
Cedar wood
Split kiawe logs
Banana log
Banana leaves
Tea leaves
Chicken wire
Wet burlap sacks
Dirt—lots of dirt!
A wooden post that is two to three feet tall
A sheet of *thick* plastic large enough to cover the whole imu
(If you don't have the plastic, you can use an old bed sheet)

Before you start preparing your imu, you need to soak the rocks in water for two weeks, and then let them dry out for two more weeks. If there's moisture inside the rocks, it can create steam, and cause the rocks to blow up (even if you use rocks with holes).

Once your rocks are prepared, it takes about an hour and a half to set up an imu. Your cooking time will be about six hours to cook three hundred pounds of kalua pig. For anything less, you'll have to estimate how long you should cook it.

It is better to use pork butts instead of a whole pig. That way, there isn't as much waste and there's less fat. If you use a whole pig, it can be very messy because of all of the oil.

The early Hawai'ians used cedar wood as kindling, and kiawe wood to make a hot fire. The kiawe went on top of the kindling.

To prepare the imu, first lay the kindling on the bottom of the pit over a layer of crumpled newspaper. Kindling is small pieces of wood that aren't too thick and can catch fire easily.

Preparing Pork for an Imu

Next, place the post in the middle of the pit, standing up straight, about two or three feet tall. To keep it balanced, situate some kiawe wood around the base of the post. (You'll learn what to do with the post later on.)

Stack more kiawe logs on top of the kindling. The kiawe logs should be split before placing them in the pit; otherwise they will take too long to burn. To stack the wood, lay it down all in one direction, then place a second layer going in the opposite direction. Leave some space between the logs for the air to flow through. For any type of fire to burn, you need fuel and oxygen. If you stack your wood layers all in the same direction, they will fall in on each other and the air won't be able to get to the flames.

Next, stack the rocks that you pre- pared over the top of the logs, piling them up so that, when you are finished, your imu looks like a stone igloo. Set aside a good sized rock– you will need it lat- er. Make sure that the tip of the post is

poking out the top far enough so that you can remove it.

Once your rock igloo is made, remove the post and either throw a match into the hole where the post was, or light a piece of crumpled newspaper and drop it into the hole. Cover the hole with the rock that you set aside earlier.

Let the fire burn until the wood is just coals. At that point, you have to level out your imu and get your rocks to lay flat on the top, so that you can pile more things on top.

After you have leveled your rocks, take a banana log and cut it into multiple short pieces (about sixteen inches long each). Split the pieces in half and pound them with a rock to loosen them up; this makes it so that the steam can go through them. Lay the banana stumps in a flat layer over the rocks, covering everything.

After you have the banana stumps in the imu, cover them with banana leaves. Then, put down a layer of clean tea leaves over the banana leaves.

Now it is time to prepare baskets for the pork. You make it out of the chicken wire. The baskets in the photo below are also lined with ti leaves.

Lay the baskets of pork in the imu and cover everything with another layer of tea leaves. Then place a layer of wet burlap sacks on top.

Finally, cover the whole thing with a sheet of thick plastic. Pile dirt around the edges of the plastic to hold it in place and to prevent the steam from escaping. You could use a bed sheet instead of plastic, but in that case you will need to cover the whole imu with dirt. With the plastic, you can just cover the edges.

By now you should have a mountain! Watch the imu as it's cooking to make sure that no steam is leaking out. If you see steam leaking out, put on more dirt and wet it down with water. If it is not completely sealed, oxygen will get through to the

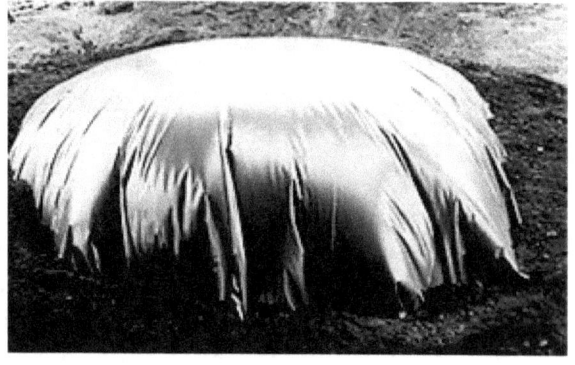

fire and create flames (which you do not want).

— Plastic sheet
— Wet burlap sacks
— tea leaves
— Pork in chicken wire basket
— tea leaves
— Banana leaves
— Banana stump
— rocks
— Pole
— Split wood
— kindling
— Crumpled newspaper

Let your pig cook for at least six hours. You don't have to cook smaller portions quite as long, but you should cook it at least for four hours. If your pork hasn't cooked in eight hours, you have done something wrong and *it will not cook*.

Once your pork is cooked, take it out of the imu and shred it. Your pork should shred easily on its own if you pull it.

You can also cook other things in the imu along with your pork, such as vegetables, other meats, or pretty much anything you want. Hawai'ian sweet potatoes are a favorite addition to a lu'au. If you add them to your imu, be sure to poke holes in the skins first to prevent them from exploding!

A Whole Pig Being Removed From an Imu
Courtesy of the Kamehameha Hotel

If you would like to have kalua pork at a lu'au, and can't make an imu, you can always make it in a slow cooker. Take a pork butt and rub it generously with Hawaiian salt. Then add liquid smoke (following the amount per pound indicated on the bottle) and cook it in a crock pot for several hours or all day. If you're doing it in a pot on the stove, it could be done in four or five hours, simmering slowly. You just add more liquid if needed. Once it's done cooking, take it out and shred it.

On the following pages are some recipes for other common foods found at lu'aus. Hawai'i has a large Asian population which has had a strong influence on its cuisine. The last two recipes are Asian dishes that have become lu'au favorites.

Lomi Lomi Salmon

- Pre-cut salted salmon
- Water to soak in
- About 2 tomatoes, chopped
- About 1 yellow onion, chopped
- 5 cubes of ice

For Lomi Lomi salmon, buy the pre-cut salted salmon that comes in a sealed bag. Soak the salmon for five minutes to get *some* of the salt off; it still needs to be salty. Add the chopped tomatoes and onions, and then mix everything together. Finally, add the ice and let it melt so the Lomi Lomi salmon is a little watery.

Haupia
(Coconut pudding cubes)

- 2 cups coconut milk
- 1/2 cup sugar
- 1/2 cup cornstarch
- 3/4 cup water

Mix the corn starch and sugar together, then add the water and stir until everything is dissolved completely. Let it sit.

Take the coconut milk, put it in a big pot on the stove, and heat it up. Stir your corn starch mixture one more time and add it to your coconut milk. Keep stirring vigorously the *whole* time you are cooking. Coconut milk burns *very* easily, so even if you stop stirring for just a moment, it may burn.

Stir until the mixture has thickened and pour into an 8 x 8 inch pan. Cool until it is room temperature and then refrigerate for at least four hours until firm. Cut into one inch squares. Keep refrigerated until you serve it.

Chicken Teriyaki

- 1/4 cup minced onions
- 1 T dried ginger
- 1/3 cup cooking wine (any type)
- 1/2 cup brown sugar
- 1/2 cup white sugar
- 2 cloves garlic
- 2 cups soy sauce
- 6 chicken pieces (breasts, thighs, or wings)

Mix all of the ingredients together, except for the chicken. Put the chicken pieces into a baking dish and pour the mixture over them. Cook at 375 degrees until done. If the pieces aren't completely covered by the sauce, turn them over once in a while as they cook.

Chicken Long Rice
(Long rice is actually a bean noodle)

- 3 lbs. chicken pieces (either with or without bones)
- 2 1/2 t salt
- 1 t garlic powder
- 1 onion, chopped
- 1 piece of ginger, crushed
- 2 cans of chicken broth
- 2 packages of long rice

Sauté the chicken pieces in a large pot with salt, garlic, paprika, and onion. Add the ginger and chicken broth. Let it simmer for 45 minutes or until chicken is tender.

Prepare the long rice noodles by soaking them in warm water for twenty minutes. Drain the noodles in a colander, rinse them in cold water, and then cut them to shorter lengths. Add the long rice to the chicken mixture five to ten minutes before serving.

www.ingramcontent.com/pod-product-compliance
Lightning Source LLC
Chambersburg PA
CBHW070646290526
45790CB00001B/202

*9 7 8 1 4 8 3 9 3 7 5 6 4 *